Ootsa Lake Odyssey

01 02 03 04 05 20 19 18 17 16

Caitlin Press Inc.
8100 Alderwood Road,
Halfmoon Bay, BC V0N 1Y1
www.caitlin-press.com

Text and cover design by Vici Johnstone
Cover image: George and Else Seel, along with unidentified person on left, at the dock of their property on Ootsa Lake. Else Seel collection. University of Victoria Archives 4-6-41
Printed in Canada

Caitlin Press Inc. acknowledges financial support from the Government of Canada and the Canada Council for the Arts, and the Province of British Columbia through the British Columbia Arts Council and the Book Publisher's Tax Credit.

Canada Council for the Arts | Conseil des Arts du Canada | British Columbia Arts Council | Funded by the Government of Canada | Canada

Library and Archives Canada Cataloguing in Publication

Sherwood, Jay, 1947-, author
Ootsa Lake odyssey : George and Else Seel—a pioneer life on the headwaters of the Nechako Watershed / Jay Sherwood.

ISBN 978-1-987915-21-1 (paperback)

1. Seel, George, 1888-1950. 2. Seel, Else, 1894?-1974. 3. Pioneers—British Columbia—Ootsa Lake—Biography. 4. Frontier and pioneer life—British Columbia--Ootsa Lake—Biography. 5. Ootsa Lake (B.C.)—History. 6. Ootsa Lake (B.C.)—Biography. I. Title.

FC3845.O68Z48 2016 971.1'820922 C2016-903967-6

OOTSA LAKE ODYSSEY

George and Else Seel — A Pioneer Life on the Headwaters of the Nechako Watershed

Jay Sherwood

Caitlin Press

Ootsa Lake
Nechako Reservoir
In 1952, the Kenney Dam was constructed on the Nechako River to service the new Alcan aluminum smelter at Kitimat, resulting in the creation of the Nechako Reservoir and the relocation of over 75 families. The damming also linked the rivers and lakes of Ootsa, Intata, Whitesail, Chelaslie, Tetachuck, Tahtsa and Natalkuz into the reservoir with a surface area of over 90,000 hectares.
BRITISH COLUMBIA
BC 150 YEARS

This book is dedicated to all the people who lived on the headwaters of the Nechako River during the first half of the twentieth century.

Opposite: Rupert at the sign for the Nechako Reservoir in 2015. Nearby was the site of the Ootsa Lake school. Rupert married Winnie Apps, the last teacher at Ootsa Lake. Photo Jay Sherwood

Contents

This is a portion of a 1930 BC government highways map of southern British Columbia. The small square indicates the location of Wistaria on Ootsa Lake. Royal BC Museum, BC Archives Cm-c178

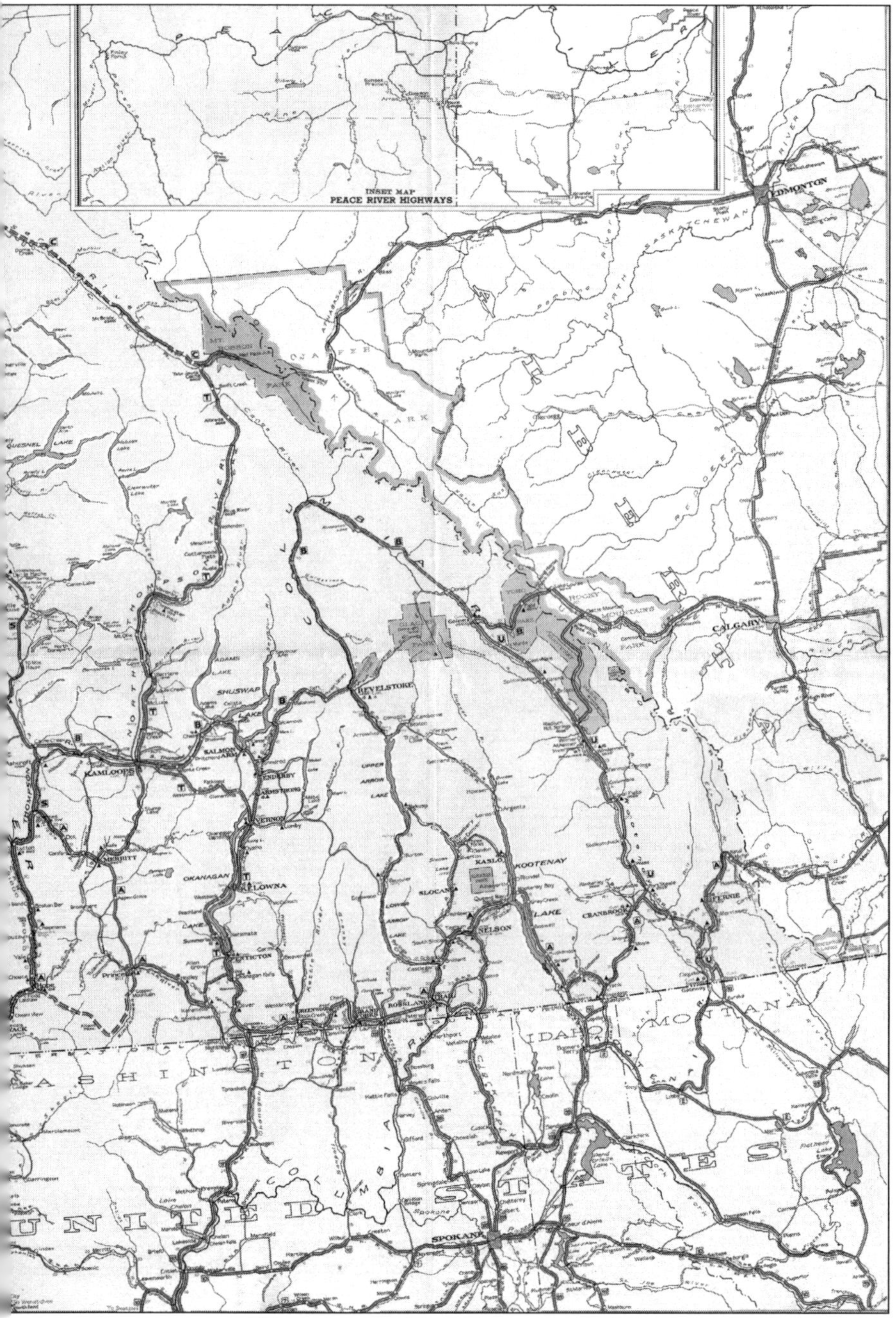
INSET MAP
PEACE RIVER HIGHWAYS
EDMONTON
NORTH SASKATCHEWAN
CALGARY
REVELSTOKE
KAMLOOPS
SHUSWAP
SALMON ARM
ENDERBY
ARMSTRONG
VERNON
KELOWNA
OKANAGAN
MERRITT
PENTICTON
KASLO
KOOTENAY
LAKE
SLOCAN
NELSON
CRANBROOK
FERNIE
ROSSLAND
TRAIL
UPPER
ARROW
LAKE
LOWER
ROCKY
MOUNTAINS
PARK
MONTANA
IDAHO
WASHINGTON
COLUMBIA
UNITED STATES
SPOKANE

Acknowledgements

Else Seel's diaries, other writing and photographs are located at the University of Victoria Archives. I would like to express my thanks to everyone on the staff there for making the materials so readily available during several research trips I made to the archives. I particularly appreciate the archives' support in providing copies of Else's photographs for this book. My thanks also go to the staff at the BC Archives for assistance with the files that I used there, particularly the location of the coroner's inquiry for William Grell. Carla Jack, Provincial Toponymist, provided information for the geographical names that related to George Seel and his early acquaintances, while the BC Legislative Library located the certificate of incorporation for the Tahtsa Mining Company.

Special thanks go to George and Else's son Rupert for his invaluable assistance. During several meetings, Rupert shared his knowledge and memories of the people and places of the Ootsa Lake area. Rupert was my guide during a July 2015 trip to the Central Interior where we visited sites around Wistaria and flew by helicopter to the mineral claims on Swing Peak that George staked in 1926. The trip provided me with a much greater understanding of the area.

During that trip, Rupert and I spent time with Mike Robertson, Senior Policy Advisor for the Cheslatta First Nation. Mike shared his knowledge of the history of the Cheslatta people, particularly as it related to George and Else, and also made accessible information from the Cheslatta gathering along the Nechako Reservoir, and it was special to be there at that time.

On that visit, Rupert and I met with Daryn Eakin, who shared his knowledge of the trapping history of the upper Nechako. I also had the opportunity to visit Chris Beach and talk about his thesis. My thanks to both of them for their assistance.

Claudia Golombiewski translated Else's diaries and other writing for this book. I appreciate the work that she did, her interest in the project, and her willingness to help whenever I requested her assistance. Claudia's knowledge of German literature was especially helpful in picking out the literary references that Else included in her diaries.

I would also like to say thank you to my wife, Linda, for her assistance, and to Vici Johnstone of Caitlin Press for publishing this book.

Arrival at Ootsa

GEORGE SEEL—FALL 1914

As they emerged from the forest, he saw Ootsa Lake for the first time. Lying at the bottom of the hill, the lake was narrow but long, and he could see only a portion of its seventy-kilometre length. In front of him and on his left, to the east, low forested mountains rose above the lake. To the right, there were high snow-covered mountains that reached above the timberline. And on the far western horizon he could see the rugged Coast Mountain range.

He was travelling with the Bolom brothers, two Swedish prospectors and trappers. World War I had started a few months before. Already the Canadian government had established internment camps to confine people who were citizens of countries like Germany, with whom it was at war, and there was a camp here in British Columbia. He claimed that he was from the United States, but he had no documentation, and with his noticeable accent, government authorities would quickly recognize that he was an enemy alien.

Although Ootsa Lake was remote, there were some settlers living there. The Bolom brothers were taking him farther, to their cabin on the Tahtsa River near the Coast Mountains, where he would learn how to trap, prospect, and live in the wilderness.

The three men continued down the hill to Ootsa Lake. Their journey would take them along the lake to its western end, then up the Tahtsa River to the area where he would remain for the rest of the war.

The road from François Lake to Ootsa Lake in the late 1920s. Ootsa Lake is in the background. Else Seel photograph. University of Victoria Archives 3-35-7

The road to Ootsa Lake in 2015. This is no longer the main road. The picture was taken closer to the lake because of the vegetation cover. Photo Jay Sherwood

ELSE SEEL—SEPTEMBER 1927

The car came out of the forest and she saw Ootsa Lake for the first time. She noticed the long, narrow lake flanked by green mountainsides and snow-capped peaks and realized the extent of the contrast between her home in Germany and the setting in front of her. She had answered an advertisement from a German-Canadian who lived at Ootsa and was seeking a wife. Leaving Berlin, she had travelled across the Atlantic Ocean by ship and across Canada by train to Vancouver. There, a day after meeting her future husband, they had married. During the next week, travel by ship, train and car had brought them to Ootsa Lake. They continued down the hill to the main settlement along the lake.

But she had not finished her journey. After staying overnight at the settlement, her husband took his boat and went ahead to prepare for her, while she accompanied a local woman who drove her to Wistaria, a small settlement farther west along the lake. There, she rejoined her husband, and they travelled in a small motorboat for a few kilometres. Rounding a point of land, they pulled into a small bay where there was a log house. She had arrived at Ootsa.

Else Seel on her initial arrival at Wistaria. University of Victoria Archives 4-6-19

Introduction

From 1905 to 1952, there was an agrarian settlement scattered across the north shore of Ootsa Lake in the Central Interior region of British Columbia. Four small community centres existed along the lake, and at its height the settlement had about three hundred people. The area, about sixty kilometres south of Burns Lake, was remote and the winters were long, but the settlers learned how to live in this environment. In the process, they developed a close connection to the land, helped each other, and established collaborative relationships with the First Nations people who lived around them.

The Seel home at the time Else married George. Ootsa Lake is in the background. Else Seel photograph. University of Victoria Archives 3-31-1

George and Else Seel and their children were part of the Ootsa Lake settlement, living near the community of Wistaria towards the western end of the lake. George was a prospector, trapper and mason who spent much of his time along the waterways and in the mountains of the Tahtsa River drainage west of Ootsa. Else was a housewife and a writer who had stories published in magazines and newspapers in her native Germany. She kept a diary that provides a record of her life at Ootsa. She also had a camera and took photographs. Else's diaries, photographs, literary works and correspondence are all preserved in the University of Victoria archives. In her later years she published a book of poems and an account of her time at Ootsa. George's prospecting activities are well documented in newspaper articles and government records.

George and Else at their log house during the late winter of 1927–28. University of Victoria Archives 3-31-5

The Seel family lived at Wistaria during the prosperous years of the 1920s and coped with the Great Depression of the 1930s. They spent some of the time during World War II at Fort St. James while George worked at the Pinchi Mine, but afterwards they returned to Ootsa Lake and adapted to life in a post-war world. George died in 1950, but Else and her son Rupert remained at Wistaria until the beginning of the Kenney Dam construction. This dam created the Nechako Reservoir, which raised the level of Ootsa Lake and flooded the Seel's property. Else, along with other landowners along Ootsa Lake, and the Cheslatta First Nation (who were affected by the establishment of the Skins Spillway), were displaced and forced to leave the land where they had lived.

Primary sources have been used as much as possible in *Ootsa Lake Odyssey*. Through these documents, we are able to view life at the Ootsa Lake settlement, and see the different perspectives of Else and George's world.

House in the Primeval Woods
Else Seel

House in the primeval woods, log on log,
Sun, moon and every star
Forming heaven's cupola
To the northern lights afar.

Earth rolls off its seasons,
Wars begin and end;
Humanity in this small place
Makes its strongest stand.

Simple life, and little house,
Things will never greater be;
Human love and pain
Grow from joy and tears eternally.

Welcome honored guest, come in,
Here you will be gladly greeted.
Wherever you have gone in life,
Here you will be friendly treated.

HAUS IM URWALD
Else Seel

Haus im Urwald, Stamm an Stamm,
Sonne, Mond und all Sterne
woelben einem Himmels Kuppeldamm
bis zum Nordlicht in die Ferne.

Erde spinnet ab die Jahreszeiten,
Kriege kommen und vergehn;
hier im Raum, in kleinen Weiten
bleibt die Menschlichkeit bestehn.

Einfach Leben, Haus und Sein,
Du kannst keine Dinge groesser machen;
Menschenlust und Menschenpein
waschen nur aus Weinen und aus Lachen.

Hier wirst Du mit Freud empfangen,
ein geehrter Gast, tritt ein.
Wohin immer Du gegangen,
hier wirst Du wilkommen sein.

The Land and the People

The Fraser River is the longest river contained entirely within British Columbia. Its headwaters originate on the western slopes of the Rocky Mountains southwest of Jasper, and the river flows west through Mount Robson Provincial Park. At Tête Jaune Cache, the Fraser leaves the Rockies and enters the Rocky Mountain Trench, where it flows northwest. About fifty kilometres before reaching Prince George, the river leaves the trench and turns towards the south.

At Prince George, the Nechako River, the second-largest tributary of the Fraser, enters from the west. The Nechako basin is the traditional homeland of the Dakelh people (formerly called Carrier). Following the route of the Nechako upstream, a person would proceed west from Prince George for about 150 kilometres, passing the community of Vanderhoof and the small settlement of Fort Fraser. At Fort Fraser, about two kilometres before Fraser Lake, the Nechako turns to the southwest.

Before the Kenney Dam was constructed in the early 1950s, one could follow the river upstream for about a hundred kilometres through the Grand Canyon of the Nechako. Not far upstream from the Grand Canyon was Natalkuz Lake. Above this lake, the river split into two long branches, both flowing into Natalkuz at the western end.

The south branch led upstream through Euchu and Tetachuck lakes to Eutsuk Lake, which headed in a northwest direction. Between Tetachuck and Eutsuk is the Redfern Rapids, the only rapids on the original upper section of the Nechako watershed. The rapids and Eutsuk Lake (which is about eighty kilometres long) are the only part of the waterway that was not directly impacted by the Nechako Reservoir created by the Kenney Dam. The western part of Eutsuk lies at the base of the Coast Range Mountains and there are passes that lead from the lake through this range.

A view of the western part of Ootsa Lake from the benchland above the lake. Else Seel photograph. University of Victoria Archives 4-6-37

The north branch went from Natalkuz Lake to Intata Lake, and up the Ootsa River to Ootsa Lake. Near the western end of Ootsa, the direction of the lake turned southwest. The Tahtsa River flowed into the western end of Ootsa. This river, about sixty kilometres long, originated at the outlet of Tahtsa Lake. From the western end of the lake it was only about five kilometres to Penteuch Pass, a route through the Coast Range to Kemano on the Pacific Ocean along Gardner Canal.

A few kilometres up the Tahtsa River, the north branch continued in a southwesterly direction. Shortly above the Tahtsa River was Sinclair (Flat) Lake, the smallest lake on the upper Nechako waterway. Upstream from Sinclair, the Whitesail River connected to Whitesail Lake. From Portage Bay, along the southeast shore of Whitesail Lake, it was about two kilometres to St. Thomas Bay on Eutsuk Lake, and a portage connected the two lakes. This created the "Great Circle," a route around the headwaters of the upper Nechako that was about 325 kilometres long and only had portages at Redfern Rapids and between Whitesail and Eutsuk lakes. In the twentieth century, the Great Circle became a popular tourist destination. Billy McNeill, one of the two Class A guides in the Ootsa area, operated Circle Guides, which specialized in hunting and fishing trips along the Great Circle route. George Seel worked for McNeill on some of his trips.

The headwaters of the Nechako are the traditional territory of the Cheslatta Carrier Nation, who are part of the Dakelh people. In the nineteenth

The famous BC land surveyor and cartographer Frank Swannell made this map of the upper Nechako watershed in 1923 after surveying the area from 1920 to 1922. The map shows the Great Circle of lakes along with Cheslatta Lake. Land Title Survey Authority 3T255

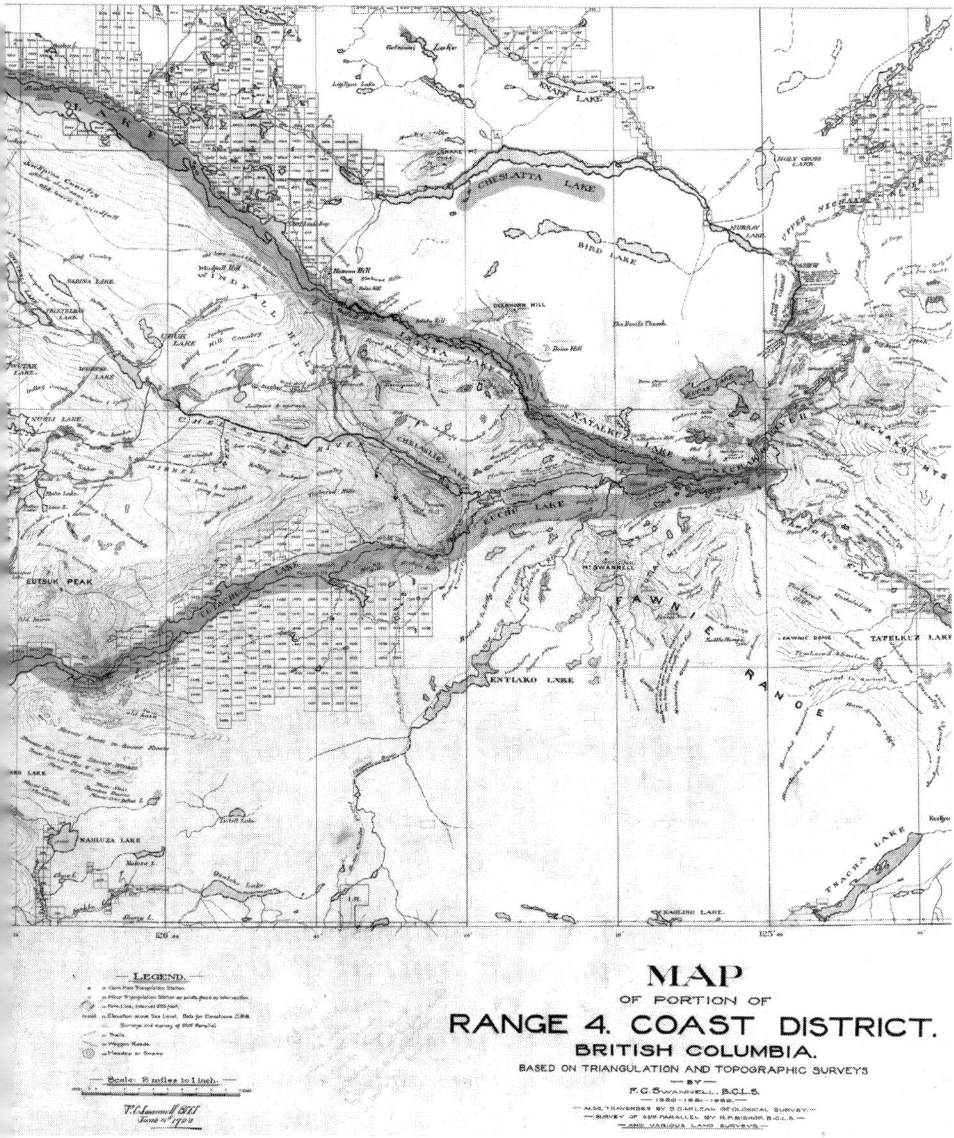
MAP
OF PORTION OF
RANGE 4. COAST DISTRICT.
BRITISH COLUMBIA.
BASED ON TRIANGULATION AND TOPOGRAPHIC SURVEYS
BY
F. C. SWANNELL, B.C.L.S.
1920-1921-1922.
LEGEND.
Scale: 2 miles to 1 inch.
CHESLATTA LAKE
KNAPP LAKE
HOLY CROSS LAKE
MURRAY LAKE
BIRD LAKE
UPPER NECHAKO RIVER
OELRHORN HILL
WINDFALL HILLS
NATALKUZ LAKE
CHELASLIE RIVER
EUCHU LAKE
MT SWANNELL
FAWNIE RANGE
NECHAKO MTS
EUTSUK PEAK
ENTIAKO LAKE
FAWNIE DOME
TATELKUZ LAKE
TSACHA LAKE
NAHLUZA LAKE
KASLINO LAKE
SABINA LAKE
126°
125°

Frank Swannell took this photograph of a group of Cheslatta people at one of their reserves on Cheslatta Lake in 1911. George and Else knew several of the people in this photograph. In the back centre is Chief Louie. On his left (facing the camera) is his son Jimmy followed by Johnny Skin (wearing a vest), White Eye Jack, Tommy Skin, and his younger brother, Robert Skin (in a white shirt). In the front, by the snowshoes, is Baptiste Louie, Chief Louie's younger brother. Kneeling, and behind him, is Skin Tyee. Skin Tyee's wife, Harriet, is sitting on the ground in front of, and to the right of Chief Louie. On her right, holding a child, is Baptiste's wife. Royal BC Museum, BC Archives I-33169

and first half of the twentieth centuries, their main residence was around Cheslatta Lake. The lake lay along a well-used First Nations transportation route (often called grease trails because they were used to bring oolichan oil from the Pacific coast). This route went from Bella Coola on the central coast, through the Coast Range to the First Nations village of Algatcho. There, another grease trail headed east, following the Blackwater River (the route Alexander Mackenzie used on his 1793 journey). The trail heading north passed through Cheslatta Lake, proceeded to Fraser Lake, and continued to the First Nations community at Stuart Lake.

In the early nineteenth century, the Hudson's Bay Company established trading posts at Fort St. James on Stuart Lake and at Fort Fraser on the eastern shore of Fraser Lake. The Cheslatta traded with the post at Fort Fraser, bringing in furs and food in exchange for trade goods. From Cheslatta Lake, the First Nations people had ready access to salmon fishing on the upper Nechako River below the Grand Canyon, the upper limit of the salmon migration. There was a portage trail from Cheslatta Lake to Ootsa Lake. Although they did not have any villages on the Great Circle route in the twentieth century, the Cheslatta used the area as part of their seasonal cycle of trapping, hunting, fishing and food gathering. (It appears that there were permanent villages on the Great Circle until the first smallpox epidemics of the nineteenth century.)

In the nineteenth century, a few non-Aboriginal people travelled through the Ootsa Lake area. When the Canadian Pacific Railway was searching for a port on the Pacific, they sent Charles Horetzky in 1874 to examine the feasibility of a route through Penteuch Pass. However, the route was not suitable.

The first settlers came to Ootsa Lake in 1905. Most of them arrived originally from Bella Coola, following the First Nations trail into the area. When construction of the Grand Trunk Pacific Railway started a couple of years later, many settlers started taking steamboats to Hazelton on the Skeena River and from there travelled overland to Ootsa. Some also arrived from the Cariboo, following the Yukon Telegraph Trail to the Burns Lake area. Many of these early settlers came from the United States, some from eastern Canada. There were also people from England and a few from other European countries, particularly from the Scandinavian region. These settlers came mainly for agricultural land, taking up pre-emptions on south-facing slopes along the north shore of Ootsa Lake. Their homesteads were located along almost the entire lake. Most were by the shore, but some people acquired land on the benches above the lake, wherever water was available. Settlement mainly revolved around four communities: Marilla, near the east end of the lake, close to the portage trail to Cheslatta Lake; Ootsa Lake, the main community, located at the end of the route that headed south from Burns Lake and across François Lake; Streatham, a small community about twenty kilometres west of Ootsa Lake; and Wistaria, about thirty kilometres from the main Ootsa settlement, and about fifteen kilometres from the western end of the lake. When George Seel first arrived at Ootsa in 1914, there were about twenty homesteads along the lake.

In 1998 Christopher Beach wrote: "Beneath the Waters: A Microhistory of Ootsa Lake, a Northern Eurocanadian Community" for his master's degree thesis at the University of Northern British Columbia. In the introduction he states that his thesis is:

> a study of how the euroCanadians who created and sustained the rural settlements of Wistaria, Streatham, Ootsa and Marilla, came to be attached to and dependent upon their environment in numerous ways over the course of five decades. It seems

> any focus on multi-generational non-natives in the provincial North has been overshadowed—if not largely ignored—at the expense of an almost microscopic examination of the transient, capitalistic euroCanadian in northern British Columbia... The transient, capitalistic characteristics of the stereotypical northern fur trader, miner, fisher and the logger appear to have consumed the imagination of many British Columbia historians in the twentieth century. The purpose of this study of Ootsa Lake is to suggest different historical possibilities for the cultural-ecological experience of non-natives in twentieth century northern British Columbia.

As part of his research, Beach conducted a structured interview with twenty-six residents of the original community, including Rupert Seel, George and Else's son.

Beach describes the evolution of the settlers who lived along the lake to the reality of their situation and their accommodation to the place where they lived.

A view of the Nechako Reservoir in 2015 taken from the benchland. This was the location where Ootsa Lake turned from the west to the southwest direction. Windy Point protrudes on the centre left, and the Coast Mountains are in the background. Photo Jay Sherwood

> Although many of the first Ootsa Lake settlers came to the region with visions of economic grandeur unattainable in the places they were leaving behind, ultimately the four Ootsa Lake settlements abandoned notions of swift prosperity as they struggled to sustain themselves in a place and time that allowed for little else. Geographic isolation gradually and persuasively ended any expectations of material wealth. Predominantly subsistence farmers, trappers and guides, the residents of Wistaria, Streatham, Ootsa and Marilla came to value quality of life and environment above financial success. The mere continuity of the community over five decades is reflective of the commitment and attachment to the way of life and economic subsistence the surrounding landscape provided.

Beach also notes the attachment and sense of place that the residents developed over the years.

> In spite of their initial intentions, the Ootsa Lake settlers did not rapidly accumulate wealth in a desperate land grab or short-term employment opportunity. Rather, these euroCanadians gradually built up farms, ranches, and guiding outfits over a period of several decades. Transiency was not a dominant factor in Ootsa Lake, as a "sense of place" developed both individually and collectively within the community across generations. The families and bachelors that settled in the area and remained through to the demise of the community at mid-century, did so with an awareness that their environment and economic livelihood would not deliver considerable material wealth, and that extensive transformation of their landscape would, in all probability, not occur.

Beach contends that most historians tended to take an economically based, monolithic view of communities in northern British Columbia. He counters that "within the region as a whole there exists an assortment of communities of divergent sizes, geographies and ecologies. The uniquely diverse environments of the Peace River District, the Interior Plateau, and the Northwest Coast have arguably precipitated equally diverse non-aboriginal cultural landscapes." The settlement at Ootsa Lake was not unique, but provided a good example of an early non-Aboriginal community in the Central Interior that existed for multiple generations and was multi-dimensional.

In summarizing the main premise of his thesis, Beach writes:

> In sum, northern, multi-generational, non-aboriginals have arguably been marginalised in much of the non-popular writing of British Columbia history. When they have been addressed, they have often been portrayed as temporary visitors in an unknown geography, imperialistically driven capitalists, as individuals possessing traits more reflective of traditional northern folklore than contemporary reality, or exclusively through their relationship with First Nations. The historical experience of the Ootsa Lake settlements breaks with these deterministic notions and much of the conventional academic wisdom of non-aboriginal communities in several ways.

Beach describes the framework of the Ootsa Lake settlement.

> As a result of their geographic location, the settlements were isolated from commercial agriculture, lumber and mining markets to a considerable degree... Residents sustained themselves through mixed farming, small-scale ranching, seasonal trapping and guiding in Tweedsmuir Park; the community was not governed by distant capital markets, the infamous boom and bust economic cycle, or the extraction of minerals or timber. Geographically isolated from even regional commercial outposts, little wage labour and currency made its way into the area. Much of the agricultural goods produced were consumed within the community itself, as transportation costs often prohibited shipping livestock to outside markets. The absence of currency became augmented by a system of bartering for non-wage labour, harvested crops, wild meat and hand-made materials.

As part of sustaining the community, the residents developed the basic cultural institutions. Beach recorded that "In addition to serving the various needs of local residents, schools, post offices, general stores, organizations, the church and the community hall all testify to the fact that this was a real, viable permanent community with a long-term outlook for the future." Their social interactions were also important. Beach went on to comment that "As much as these people were dependent upon the environment, and shaped their lives around that relationship, the settlers of Ootsa Lake were dependent upon one another for recreation, sustenance, friendship, social interaction and economy." Beach notes that as a result:

> The people of Ootsa Lake learned early on to sustain themselves from the abundance of the surrounding environment, as they cultivated domestic crops, harvested natural ones, and relied on few cultural amenities and consumer products. Geography and distance left them little choice, shutting the settlers off from regional labour and commercial markets. Subsisting largely independent from "the outside" residents produced all kinds of goods that would normally be bought from a store.

The remains of the Bob Nelson home in 2015. This building also served as the Wistaria post office and the teacherage was upstairs. Photo Jay Sherwood

Besides the residents' dependence on their local environment to sustain them:

> the primary cash earning occupations in the community, farming, trapping and guiding, all depended upon the conservation of the environment and limited transformation of the surrounding landscape, particularly when compared to northern mining or logging "company" towns that precipitated the massive transformation of [their] immediate surroundings. In this context, Ootsa Lake residents as a whole offer an historiographically unconventional impression of northern, twentieth century, British Columbia communities.

Beach comments that "without exception, not a single person interviewed, nor any individual they could remember, accumulated considerable sums of money at Ootsa Lake."

Beach focuses primarily on the interaction of the settlers among themselves and only provides a few references to relations with the local First Nations people. In one of Beach's interviews, Jim Van Tine described how bartering also applied to trade relationships with the First Nations people.

He noted that the Skins family:

> ... used to come over and help, work for vegetables... helped fence, or dig potatoes, or hoe the garden... Chief Louie, when he used to go through trapping in the spring, he'd come up here pulling a big dug-out canoe, his whole family with him going up to Tahtsa [Lake]. And he'd stop with... what women made in the wintertime, moccasins and gloves and jackets, and trade for turnips... jams once in a while... They'd just trade, money didn't mean anything.

For the summer/fall 2003 edition of *BC Studies*, Soren Larsen wrote an article titled "Collaboration Geographies: Native-White partnerships during the Re-settlement of Ootsa Lake, British Columbia, 1900–1952." In this article, Larsen expands on Beach's thesis by applying many of his premises to the relationship between the Ootsa Lake settlers and the local First Nations people. Larsen explains the main premise of his article:

> Its central argument is that, although European residents and the Cheslatta T'en First Nation maintained a social and geographical distance, certain families established longstanding interethnic collaborations that continue to play a significant role in regional politics today. On the simplest level, the region's limited resource base and market isolation meant that Whites and the Cheslatta benefited from collaborating with regard to work, information exchange, and trade.
>
> At the same time, the colonial administration in Victoria had great difficulty asserting its authority in the region. Consequently, settlers and Aboriginals struggled over the local allocation of power. During this process, some immigrant and indigenous residents found that they were able to enhance economic and social rewards within their own communities by forging collaborative relationships across ethnic lines. In turn, these family partnerships weakened—but did not eradicate the colonial idea and practice of segregation. The two factions thus created a complex society that simultaneously reproduced and challenged the social and cultural order of colonialism.

Like Beach, Larsen used structured interviews with twenty-two settlers and seventeen Cheslatta Elders as an important part of his research. He found that thirteen Cheslatta mentioned conflicts with non-Aboriginal people, but only four identified specific individuals. Twelve settlers noted conflict with the Cheslatta and eight mentioned specific individuals. In contrast, fourteen Cheslatta individuals named specific settlers with whom they collaborated and eighteen settlers named Cheslatta individuals with whom they had partnerships. Larsen commented that "Although aboriginal and white women did identify such partnerships, all interviewees indicated that the collaborations occurred between men involved in the pursuit of trade, information exchange, and labour. Interviewees also revealed that most of these collaborations (88 per cent) were stable and exclusive associations between two male heads of family."

Larsen notes that in the interviews "sixteen Cheslatta and White respondents indicated that their families had forged exclusive trading partnerships, which proved to be especially valuable during the periodic episodes of resource scarcity." Not only were these working relationships, they sometimes led to long-term friendships. He comments: "These relationships were not ephemeral but, rather, were genuine partnerships that typically lasted lifetimes." He contends:

> A complex dynamic of subordination and socio-cultural exchange characterized colonial life in the Ootsa Lake region. On the one hand, land appropriation and the frontier cultural complex promoted the development of a distinct and privileged society for European settlers...
>
> At the same time, Ootsa Lake settlers found themselves depending on the Cheslatta people for food, trade goods, and geographical information about the new environment. This dependence allowed the Cheslatta to maintain a measure of control as they both resisted and accommodated colonial resettlement. In short, the shared predicament of living in an isolated and often harsh environment generated opportunities for social collaboration. In particular, Aboriginal and White men cultivated interethnic relationships in order to augment economic productivity and to enhance social prestige within their own communities. In so doing, they weakened both the conception and reality of a segregated colonial existence.

The collaboration between the Cheslatta and the settlers continued and evolved over the years. Larsen notes that "guiding was a major interethnic undertaking in the region. The business developed during the 1920s and provided much-needed cash income for Aboriginal and settler families." Twelve residents acquired guiding licences and "most of these entrepreneurs worked directly with Cheslatta men to help plan the trips, pack the horses, track game, and entertain the hunters."

Larsen believes that collaboration between the settlers and the Cheslatta had an impact on the traditional relationship between the two groups of people living in the area. He claims that "Ultimately, this intertwined social reality diminished—but did not eradicate—the ethnic segregation promoted by colonialism. Leaders from both groups tried to avert territorial conflict in order to preserve the mutual benefits they derived from collaboration."

In his conclusion, Larsen writes:

> Social life in the Ootsa Lake region reproduced and reworked colonialism's geographies of exclusion. The overarching force of colonial resettlement, of course, created and constantly reinforced the social, cultural, and physical boundaries of otherness. Yet settlers and Aboriginals had to collaborate, negotiate, and communicate with one another because their region was so detached from the reach of colonial administration and the integrative effects of modern economic markets. Ultimately, the

The Seel residence was in a shallow bay along Ootsa Lake, so their house was in the present-day reservoir about 400 metres from the shoreline. The location was in a windy area, where there were often waves on the lake. Photo Jay Sherwood

> region's isolation gave rise to a system of establishing status through interethnic collaboration that, at times, challenged the practice of segregation. In their harsh and remote geographical setting, immigrants and Aboriginals negotiated local allocations of power through ongoing cycles of conflict and collaboration that, in the final analysis came to define social life in their region.

Larsen notes the long-standing effect of this collaboration for "the complex society formed at Ootsa Lake during the colonial period remains a significant factor in contemporary regional politics."

George and Else Seel lived about two kilometres from Wistaria, and were residents for most of the years between the first non-Aboriginal settlement at Ootsa and the flooding of the lake created by the construction of Kenney Dam and the Nechako Reservoir. They leased and eventually purchased property, built a log home, and raised their family. The Seels obtained their water from the lake and heated their house with wood. George often returned from his trips up the Tahtsa River towing logs to be cut into firewood. There was no electricity along Ootsa Lake until the second half of the twentieth century. Although some settlers later had a telephone and a few had cars, the Seels lived without these conveniences. George and Else's experiences largely reflect the opinions expressed by Beach and Larsen. They participated in both the economic and social fabric of the settlement and developed long-term friendships. They gave and received assistance from other people and had a close relationship with the world in which they lived.

George and Else collaborated with First Nations people, developing relationships with them, particularly with Baptiste and Chief Louie, who had traplines on their traditional territory in the Tahtsa River drainage. George's trapline adjoined Baptiste's. One winter, early in his years of trapping, George became very ill with scurvy. On the way to his trapline, Baptiste stopped to visit George at his cabin on the Tahtsa River. Knowing the cause of George's illness, Baptiste helped restore him to health by preparing spruce needle tea, a rich source of vitamin C. After George established a residence on Ootsa Lake, Baptiste and his family often camped on the Seel property when they were travelling between Cheslatta Lake and the Tahtsa area and the two families would visit and sometimes barter goods. George and Else also had contact with Jimmy Andrews (a Wet'suwet'en First Nation man) and his family, who lived at the west end of Ootsa Lake.

But George and Else's experiences also illustrate the diversity that existed within the settlement along Ootsa Lake. For almost all of the people who lived there, agriculture was part of their economic livelihood, and it was the primary reason they settled in the area. George's main sources of income were trapping and prospecting, supplemented by casual work for other people around the settlement. He was the only person in the Wistaria area with masonry skills. George also worked occasionally with Billy McNeill from the Ootsa settlement, assisting with his guiding business or his government contracts to keep the Tahtsa River safe for boat travel. Whether it was his personality, or a result of the years spent in isolation in the Tahtsa during World War I, George was happiest and spent most of his time in the mountains, trapping in the winter and prospecting in the summer.

The family had a garden, grew a large amount of food, and built a root cellar. George usually shot a moose for meat.

The boat was the family's main form of transportation. George never had a car, and the family didn't have horses until after World War II. This made travel particularly difficult for Else, for when George was away she had to walk everywhere or rely on other people for transportation.

There were only a few people of German origin around Ootsa Lake or in the area north towards François Lake, so the Seels were part of a small ethnic community. Else in particular maintained contact with the German-speaking people in the region.

Else came from a different background than most of the women around Ootsa Lake. She had lived in Berlin, where she had been part of the literary community, and was a published writer. At Wistaria, she maintained contact with this community through letters to friends and family and magazines that she received from Germany. There are occasional literary references in Else's diaries. She was an avid reader and wrote short stories and poems that were published in newspapers and magazines in Germany. Most of Else's writing revolved around the people that she met at Ootsa or her personal experiences.

Else and her literature have been the subject of several articles. (She is also featured in *Unter Dunklen Wassen,* a fictional book written in German by Bernadette Calonego, that has been translated into English with the title *Under Dark Waters.*) Her writing is considered part of German-Canadian literature and is mentioned in the *Canadian Encyclopedia* in an article titled "German Writing," where Walter Riedel states: "Else Seel wrote poetry, short prose and a diary reminiscent of the work of Catharine Parr Traill and Susanna Moody." After leaving Ootsa, Else published a book of poems in German, *Haus im Urwald (House in the Primeval Forest)*, and a book, *Kanadisches Tagebuch*, later published in English as *Canadian Diary*. The book recounts Else's experiences at Ootsa Lake. The intended audience for her writing was people in German-speaking countries in Europe.

Rodney Symington, a professor of German studies at the University of Victoria, wrote about Else's literature in an essay: "The published version of her *Canadian Diary* is the result of selecting, rewriting, reordering and shaping her diaries: in brief, it is a conscious work of art with a definite format infused with a consistent view." He also comments that "the immediacy of the original diary entries is, so to speak, recollected in tranquility."

Most of the stories that Else published in magazines and newspapers in Germany were based on people she knew (who were given fictionalized names) or on events that occurred to her. Else received payment for this work, and it provided some income for the family. Her mother had money, and she was able to provide some financial assistance to Else, particularly during the Depression. Else travelled more than most of the women in the area. She took two trips back to Germany in the 1930s, and on a few occasions travelled to places in northern BC. But while George was happiest in the mountains, Else was most content at the house when she was at Ootsa Lake. Only on a couple of occasions did she accompany George on trips to places in the wilderness around them.

Else kept a diary and wrote about her life at Ootsa. She described both the joy of living there and the frustration that she felt at times, particularly during the difficult economic conditions of the Depression. At times she was lonely, especially when George was away, and at other times she revelled in being alone. She felt a connection to the land, but occasionally she felt that her sense of place bound her too tightly. She felt liberated from the cultural and gender restrictions she had experienced in Europe, but at times chafed under the limited opportunities for work and the necessity of assuming a traditional woman's role of caring for the house and family.

Yet despite her occasional ambivalence, once she left Berlin, Ootsa was her home and it remained the centre of her life for twenty-five years until their property was flooded by the Nechako Reservoir during the Alcan project. Although George left only a few letters, by all accounts he felt no ambivalence: Ootsa and the surrounding wilderness was home for him. Once he arrived during World War I, the only time that George left was when he worked at Pinchi Mine during World War II. He spent thirty-five years around Ootsa Lake and is buried in the small Wistaria graveyard.

Wistaria

Wistaria, the second-largest settlement along Ootsa Lake, had many of the institutions common to small remote communities in the BC Interior. There was a community hall for group activities, a church, and a one-room elementary school that never had more than twenty students. The post office was located at the home of Bob Nelson, the postmaster. Mail arrived a couple of times a week and provided an opportunity for people to visit each other. There was a small store at Wistaria for a few years, but the population of the area was not large enough to sustain it. People were largely self-sufficient and the items that they needed were usually purchased from the Schreiber store at the main settlement at Ootsa or ordered by mail.

The population of Wistaria remained fairly constant between 1920 and 1950. The 1921 census listed eighty-five people living at the community. The 1923 voters' list had fifty adults for Wistaria and Streatham. The 1935 voters' list included fifty-five adults at Wistaria, eleven of them members of the Harrison family. In 1940 there were fifty-one voters, including eleven members of the Harrison family. In 1949 there were fifty-five adult voters registered; about a third of them were members of the Harrison family and almost a quarter belonged to the Shelford family. On all these lists, George Seel stated that his occupation was prospector. At its maximum, the population of Wistaria was probably about 125 people.

Most of the families pre-empted 160 acres [65 hectares] of land for a farm. During the first half of the twentieth century this was sufficient, for there was very little mechanization on most farms. The size of the family, and particularly the number of sons, often dictated how much land could be farmed. The settlers of the Ootsa Lake area were too far away from any markets for their products, so they raised what they needed for their personal use or to trade with other people. The farms mainly produced hay and raised beef and dairy cattle. Some had pigs. Almost every household had a large garden, and root vegetables grew particularly well. Several families raised chickens.

The largest family at Wistaria was the Harrisons, and they were among the earliest settlers, with most of them arriving before World War I. William Henry Harrison (Old Bill) was born in 1868 in Ontario. His family moved to Manitoba in the 1870s to farm. As a young man, Bill moved to Montana to become a miner, and in 1890, he married Minnie Lucille Brown in Missoula. During the next eight years, six children were born in various mining communities in Idaho. By 1899 the family had moved to the East Kootenay region, and in the 1901 census, Bill was listed as a miner and his family lived in Canterbury (present-day Invermere). Old Bill arrived in Wistaria in 1908. Altogether there were twelve children in the family, and several of them lived in Wistaria as adults. The Harrisons covered all of the main occupations—farming, trapping, prospecting and guiding, and they also had a small sawmill, one of the few industries in the area. A couple of the Harrison families had cars.

This monument was established on the grounds of the Wistaria community hall during the centennial of the establishment of the united colony of British Columbia. Photo Jay Sherwood

In the 1920s, George Seel settled at Wistaria, which was the closest settlement to the Tahtsa River area where he trapped and prospected. Initially he leased a small parcel of land from Old Bill, and then purchased six hectares of land, although he did not have it surveyed until 1946.

Old Bill and Minnie lived along the lake, less than a kilometre to the west, and they provided great assistance to Else when she first came to Wistaria. Their other close neighbour was the family of Ed Harrison, Bill's eldest son, who lived along the lake to the east, about a kilometre away. When George was home, he and Ed frequently worked together, and Else and Esther (usually called Mrs. Ed or Eddie) often visited each other for tea. The Harrisons

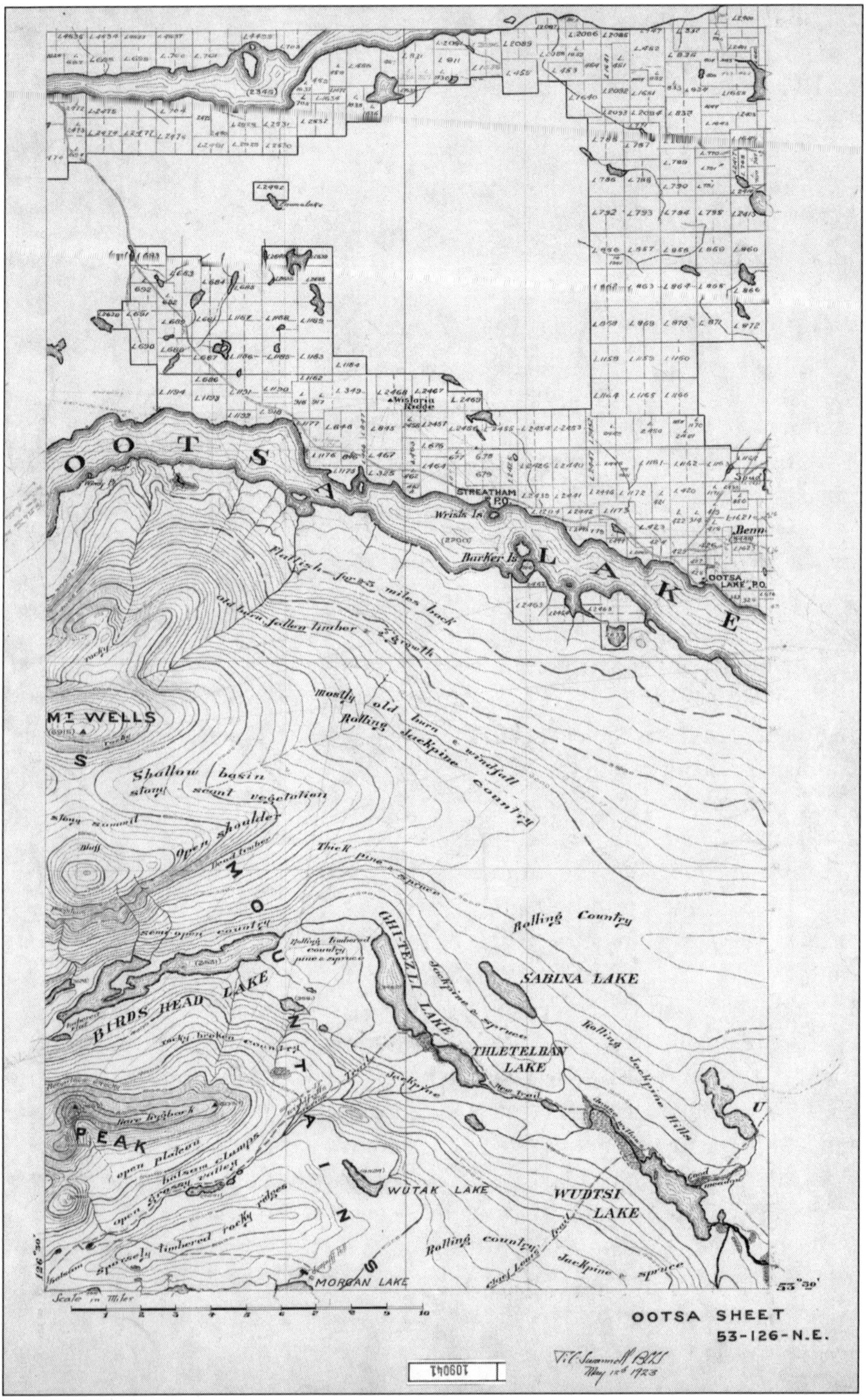
OOTSA LAKE
STREATHAM P.O.
Wrisk Is.
Barker Is.
OOTSA LAKE P.O.
Wistaria Ridge
MT WELLS
(6915)
Shallow basin
stony scant vegetation
Open shoulder
semi open country
Rolling timbered country pine & spruce
BIRDS HEAD LAKE
rocky broken country
PEAK
open plateau
balsam clumps
open grassy valley
sparsely timbered rocky ridges
Mostly old burn & windfall
Rolling Jackpine country
Thick pine & spruce
Rolling Country
SABINA LAKE
GHI-TEZLI LAKE
THLETELBAN LAKE
Rolling Jackpine Hills
WUTAK LAKE
WUDTSI LAKE
MORGAN LAKE
Rolling country
Jackpine & spruce
New trail
Scale in Miles
OOTSA SHEET
53-126-N.E.
May 12th 1923
53°30'
126°30'

The Harrison sawmill. Else Seel photograph. University of Victoria Archives 4-3-24

had a son, Ernie, who was two years older than Else and George's son, Rupert; and two girls, Esther and Irene, who were about the age of the Seels' daughter, Gloria. There were other Harrison families (sons of Old Bill and Minnie) who lived to the west, including Cliff, Buster, Bill Jr. and Orald. Alf, the second youngest son, lived with his parents until he married. One of the Harrisons' daughters, Beatrice (also called Sammie), married Paddy Carroll, and they lived on property that was the farthest west along the lake at Wistaria. Beatrice had two daughters, Cecil and Pat, who were about the same age as Rupert and Gloria. Although the Carroll family lived over six kilometres away, Else and Beatrice frequently visited each other during the 1930s. On the occasions when both George and Else were away, Rupert and Gloria usually stayed with one of the Harrison families, often with the family of Buster and Vera. Rupert recalls Alf being a mentor to him.

Opposite: Frank Swannell made this map showing land usage along the western part of Ootsa Lake. The Wistaria post office is faintly marked above L1176. The Seel property was on a portion of L1177 along the lake. Although the land along Ootsa Lake and on the bench was surveyed, not every lot was occupied. The unsurveyed land between François Lake and Ootsa was mainly forested and belonged to the Crown. Land Title Survey Authority 11T1

Inside the Harrison sawmill. Else Seel photograph. University of Victoria Archives 4-3-24

Another family with whom the Seels had frequent contact was the Mohrs. Ed and Anna were from the United States, but both of them had German parents. Else enjoyed visiting the Mohrs because they both spoke German. Initially the family lived at Wistaria, but then they moved to Streatham, about five kilometres from the Seel residence. The Mohrs mainly worked on their farm, and George sometimes helped them with haying. In the late 1930s, the Mohrs started making cheese.

Since Bob Nelson was the postmaster, Else and George often saw the Nelson family, comprised of Bob, his wife, Louise, and their daughter, Alice (who married Alf Harrison). It was about three kilometres from the Seel residence to the Nelson household. Bob was kind to Else, and during the 1930s, when the children were small and George was away from home, he sometimes brought the mail to the house and stopped to visit and help. George often used Bob's horses for ploughing the garden, and after World War II the Seels purchased some horses from Nelson.

There was one family that lived along Ootsa Lake outside Wistaria that was important to George and Else. Norm Schreiber had the contract to deliver the mail to the communities between Ootsa and François Lake. When Else travelled to places beyond Ootsa Lake, she usually began and finished her trip travelling in Norm's mail truck (or sleigh in the winter). Beginning in the

The steam donkey that the Harrisons used to power their sawmill still remains on the Wistaria community hall grounds. Photo Jay Sherwood

early 1930s, Norm Schreiber and his wife, Grace, operated a store at the main settlement at Ootsa, and George and Else purchased much of their groceries there. Norm was a fur buyer. George often sold his furs to him and used the money to pay for groceries. Norm's wife, Grace, nicknamed "the Amazon" by Else, was a former schoolteacher in the area. She and Else were good friends, even though they didn't see each other too often.

The community of Wistaria was spread out over several kilometres and there were farms both along the lake and on the benchland. The interaction that the Seel family had with some of the people at Wistaria was typical of the settlers who lived there. Distance, common or mutually beneficial interests, personality, and the age of a family's children were all factors that helped determine the people with whom each family had their closest associations.

Prosperity

George Seel was born in 1888 in Bavaria in southern Germany. His father had a small farm near the community of Flotzheim, and, as the oldest son, George would have inherited it. According to family history, George was involved in a love triangle as a young man. As a result, he was shot in the knee, a wound that would occasionally hamper him for the rest of his life. Possibly as a consequence of this incident, George left Flotzheim around 1910 and spent about a year in northern Germany before emigrating. He did not have sufficient funds to purchase a ticket on a steamship, so he stowed away on a freighter. At sea, George's presence was discovered, and he was put to work. When the ship reached Australia, George tried to leave but he was caught and returned to the freighter. At New York, George successfully jumped ship. Impoverished and homeless, he was befriended by a New York City policeman who arranged a place for George to stay and found employment for him, working for a stonemason and learning a trade.

In the summer of 1912, George left New York. A Canadian border crossing record shows that he entered Canada from Rouses Point, New York, on July 15. He declared that he was a US citizen, that his occupation was stonecutter, and that he was travelling by train to Montreal. During the following months, George made his way westward, and by 1913 he was employed on the construction of the Grand Trunk Pacific Railway in the Prince George area. In 1914, he worked in the Burns Lake area during the completion of the railway and was a section foreman when World War I started.

Since he was a German national, George knew that he would likely be arrested and sent to an internment camp, even though he claimed that he was a US citizen, so he went with the Bolom brothers to their cabin on the Tahtsa River. (Not much is known about the Bolom brothers, but they are mentioned several times in people's recollections and there are a couple of photographs of them. Although the Bolom brothers left the area before 1920, their well-built cabin was still used by people until the river was flooded by the Alcan project.) There had been a mineral rush into the Tahtsa drainage in 1913 (described in newspaper articles and the BC government's Department of Mines report), but many of the prospectors left after the war started. When British Columbia land surveyor Frank Swannell surveyed the Tahtsa drainage in 1921, he noted in his diary: "August 28th—At old camp at head of Tahtsa find names—Preston Locke, Bert T. Smith, Paul Linquist, Bob Bolom—September 9/16." Preston Locke was a prominent mining engineer for the American Smelting and Refining Company who came to British Columbia on mineral exploration trips several times.

During the war years, George trapped in the winter and did some prospecting in the summer. Some people provided assistance by selling the furs that he trapped and using the money to buy supplies for him.

In 1917, Charles Musclow came to the Tahtsa River, and during the following years his life and Seel's were connected. In 1910, Musclow and an older brother came from Ontario to the Ootsa Lake area where they spent one winter trapping. Soon after World War I started, Charles tried to enlist but was rejected because his father had been born in Germany. When conscription was proclaimed in 1917, Musclow left Ontario and rode the rails across the country to the Burns Lake area. Then he made his way to the Tahtsa River. There he built a cabin not far from the Bolom brothers' cabin and one that George had constructed for himself during the war.

Seel and Musclow trapped in the Troitsa Lake drainage that was near their cabins. In late 1919, the Canadian government proclaimed an amnesty for people who had illegally avoided their obligations during the war. In May 1920, the Prince George *Citizen* wrote an article about hunting in the Ootsa Lake country and mentioned Musclow and another trapper. The newspaper reported that "their backs are bent by the weight of muskrat and marten skins. One of them, C. A. Musclow, has been in the hills for the past three years." Seel and Musclow moved to Ootsa Lake, probably sometime in 1920, and they were joined by Musclow's younger brother, Harry. In the 1921 Canadian census, the three men are recorded as living together in the same household at Ootsa Lake. Seel is listed as the head of the household and the two brothers as lodgers. George again states that he was born in the United States, but that his parents were born in Germany.

In 1920, Frank Swannell returned to Canada after serving for almost five years in World War I and the Allied Expeditionary Force in northern Russia. Before the war, from 1912 to 1914, Swannell had done an extensive triangulation surveying and mapping project in northern British Columbia. Now the provincial government wanted him to undertake a similar surveying and mapping project on the east side of the Coast Mountains in central British Columbia. This work, which would take Swannell nine field seasons to complete, is documented in the book, *Surveying Central British Columbia: A Photojournal of Frank Swannell, 1920–1928*. During the summer of 1920, Seel and Musclow worked on his crew.

Swannell planned to start the 1920 field season surveying at Whitesail Lake. He arrived in Burns Lake at the beginning of June. There he met Charles Musclow. He noted: "Arrange with Musclow for Chestnut freight canoe & Peterboro for $1.00 per day—petrol payable by me—boat due to arrive Friday—he to get it thru to Ootsa & if required to take one ton provisions in at rate to be settled later."

From Burns Lake, Swannell's crew travelled to Ootsa Lake, and then went by boat to Whitesail Lake. After surveying around that area, the men portaged to Eutsuk Lake. By early August, Swannell had finished his work there. As part of his project, Swannell needed to make a connection to some BC government surveys done on the west side of the Coast Mountains near Kimsquit. From the southwest end of Eutsuk Lake, Swannell and his crew planned to go over Smaby Pass, down into the Kimsquit valley, and follow it to the small settlement of Kimsquit on the Pacific Ocean. There Swannell was supposed to link his surveying to work done by J. T. Underhill along Dean Channel the previous year. On August 10, Swannell's crew began cutting a trail and packing supplies from Eutsuk into Musclow (Little Eutsuk) Lake. Swannell spent a few days surveying at Musclow Lake and nearby Surel Lake.

Frank Swannell and one of his crew members, Ed Lee, both kept diaries. In his entry for August 13, Lee wrote that "George Seel came to our camp and is going to assist us in getting on with our trail as far as the fish houses... built many years ago by the Indians and used for drying salmon which they caught at the coast and brought up the range for their own use. Their old trails we find showing where hundreds of Indians inhabited the country." In his diary entry for August 14, Swannell wrote: "George Seel's time starts @ $3.50 per day."

In his government report, Swannell wrote that the First Nations trail beyond Cosgrove Lake had not been used for many years and was difficult to locate. This necessitated cutting new trail, "following the old blazes wherever traceable." By August 19, the crew reached Smaby Pass where Seel and Shorty Haven constructed a lean-to.

During the next week Swannell and his crew surveyed the surrounding area and cleared a trail towards the Kimsquit valley. Swannell wrote in his diary for August 26: "5am a drizzling rain starts—regular Coast weather—clouds & rainfall driving up the Kimsquit obscuring the peaks. George, Fort, Ed & I put to try & trace out & reblaze the old Indian trail." In the afternoon,

George Seel (left) and Shorty Haven standing by the lean-to they constructed. Frank Swannell photograph. Royal BC Museum, BC Archives I-57119

the "trail crew return sodden & soaked 2pm—Dole out the last of our Hudson Bay rum—a spoonful per man in a cup of hot coffee. Has a great effect on the morale—the glow of brotherly love & intense politeness & consideration for others lasts the day through."

Two days later Swannell made "today Sunday so that Seel may keep his appointment with Musclow." (The survey crews usually worked six days a week and had Sunday off. Occasionally, depending on weather or circumstances, the men would have their rest on a different day of the week, but they still called it Sunday. Swannell made this day a Sunday for his crew while he prepared items to send out with Seel.) Seel was meeting Musclow, who was coming from Ootsa Lake, at a designated place. Swannell wrote a letter to the surveyor general describing the progress of his survey and sent it and the crew's pay slips with Seel for Musclow to mail. Seel left in the early afternoon.

The weather improved, so while Seel was gone Swannell spent a few days surveying above the Kimsquit valley and some crew members began transporting equipment down into the Kimsquit. By September 8, the crew had

George Seel (background) and Shorty Haven using wedges to split a cedar plank. Frank Swannell photograph. Royal BC Museum, BC Archives I-57116

The split cedar plank. Frank Swannell photograph. Royal BC Museum, BC Archives I-57117

reached Camp 27 on the northeast fork of the Kimsquit River. In his diary, Lee noted Seel's return, bringing mail and tobacco for the men. Swannell described the miserable conditions: "Rain, rain all day and night. Call all work off. Seel busy splitting slabs out of a big cedar & putting up a lean-to."

In his journal for the next day Swannell wrote:

> Raining hard at 5 am—call off breakfast until 7am and stay in all morning... Push on with Shorty, Seel & Fort to "Hell's Half Acre" as Shorty terms the fetid jungle between the North Fork & Seel River—strike an old blaze but like a will o' the wisp it guides us into a beaver meadow—crosscut to the river & cut down the big spruce we bivouacked under—rig up spring-boards—takes the four of us one hour—5 foot on the stump—makes an excellent bridge... Return thoroughly drenched but satisfied with life again... The mountains show thru the clouds tonight beautiful in a tracing of new snow. The rain has washed away some of the taint of rotten salmon from the bars—but still cohoes, steelheads & humpbacks are feebly working upstream.

George Seel (left), Frank Swannell and Shorty Haven. Swannell recorded that it took four people one hour to chop down this tree, which they used as a bridge to cross the Kimsquit River. Royal BC Museum, BC Archives I-58568

Swannell's crew in the Kimsquit valley. George Seel is on the left with his wooden packboard behind him. Frank Swannell photograph. Royal BC Museum, BC Archives I-58355

During the rest of September, Swannell completed a traverse survey of about fifty kilometres down the Kimsquit valley and in the first half of October connected his survey of Whitesail and Eutsuk lakes to Underhill's survey at Dean Channel.

In 1921, Swannell continued his survey of the Coast Mountains. He spent the first part of the summer working along the coast around Kitlope Lake near the head of Gardner Canal. Then he went to Ootsa Lake, arriving there in early July. He needed some additional crew members, so he hired Charles Musclow and his brother Harry. (George must have been away in the mountains prospecting. Swannell spent most of the summer surveying in the Tahtsa River drainage, and he would have wanted Seel because of his knowledge of the area if he had met him.) In his diary entry for July 13, Swannell noted that they stayed at Musclow's cabin above the Blue River trail, a location on the Tahtsa River not far from George Seel's cabin and the Bolom cabin.

Swannell spent the entire summer of 1922 surveying the area around the Great Circle at the headwaters of the Nechako River. Once again, Charles Musclow worked on his crew. (Musclow's brother Harry had returned to Ontario. In 1923, Charles left the Ootsa area, working on a Geological Survey crew in the Northwest Territories before returning to Ontario.)

Charles Musclow (left) and his brother Harry at the outlet of Tahtsa Lake. Frank Swannell photograph. BC Archives I-57131

The following summer Swannell completed his survey of this section of the east side of the Coast Mountains. His work included a return to the Tahtsa drainage in mid-September. There he surveyed the chain of lakes and creeks of the Troitsa drainage that extended from the Tahtsa River southwest to the summit of the Coast Mountain Range. On September 16, along the lower section of the river, Swannell met George Seel: "Camp 5pm near Tahtsa River with George Seel and Bill Sweeney." The two men were probably on a prospecting trip. The next night, Swannell and his crew stayed at Musclow's cabin. On the morning of September 18, "run downstream to end of Troitsa Trail and pack across in four loads. Start to build raft but Baptiste [Louie] arriving hire his canoe." During the next ten days, Swannell's crew surveyed the drainage that contained Troitsa Lake, the Blanket Lakes, and a lake that he called Upper Blanket Lake.

Swannell made a map of his survey of the Coast Mountain area around the headwaters of the Nechako River, and as a government surveyor he was able to submit names for geographical features in the area where he worked. Among these features was Musclow Lake and Mount Musclow near Eutsuk Lake.

Opposite: Frank Swannell took this photograph of prospector Bill Sweeney in 1921. Royal BC Museum, BC Archives J-00865

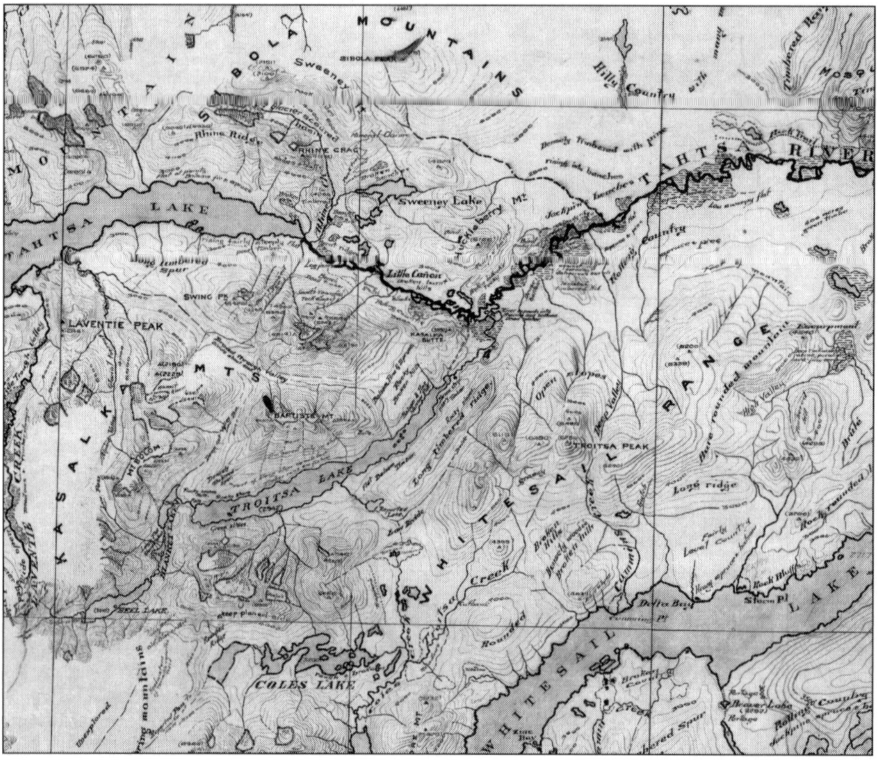

This portion of Swannell's map shows the features of the Tahtsa drainage. Land Title Survey Authority 3T255

(After Charles Musclow married in 1928, he and his bride spent a six-week honeymoon in the Ootsa Lake area and hiked to the top of the mountain named for him.) On the north side of the Tahtsa River, Swannell named Mount Sweeney and Sweeney Lake for prospector W. J. (Bill) Sweeney, an important person in George Seel's life.

On the south side of the Tahtsa, in the Troitsa drainage, Swannell provided this information for naming the Blanket Lakes: "The name was given to several small lakes west of Troitsa by trappers Seel and Musclow, who had

Opposite: This is the original sketch showing George's trapline territory. Later, George's trapline was extended to include all of Coles Lake. Seel Lake was just north of his trapline. In the early 1920s, George's trapline was adjacent to that of Michel Edmond, a member of the Cheslatta First Nation, whose traditional territory was in that area. Seel family collection.

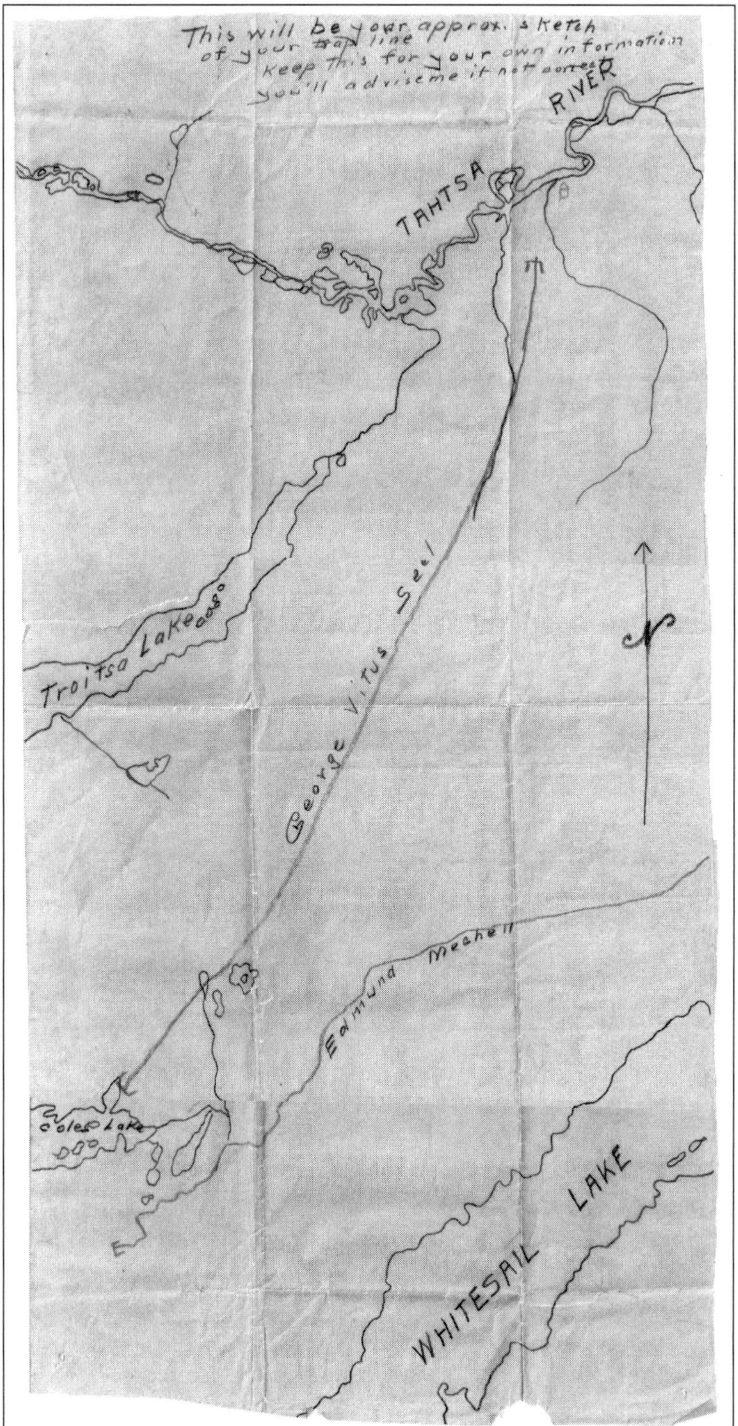
This will be your approx. sketch of your trap line
keep this for your own information
you'll adviseme if not correct
TAHTSA RIVER
Troitsa Lake
George Vitus Seel
N
Edmund Mechell
Coles Lake
WHITESAIL LAKE

discovered the lakes. They had a cache of blankets on one of them." Swannell changed the name of the upper lake to Seel Lake and provided this notation: "Named after a trapper, George Seel, who in company with Chas. Musclow was the first whiteman to explore from Troitsa Lake westward." This body of water is located just west of George's trapline area. Less than ten kilometres from Seel Lake, on the north side of Troitsa, is Mount Baptiste, named for Baptiste Louie. And above Blanket Lake, only a few kilometres distant, Mount Bolom ("an established name referring to an old prospector," according to Swannell) looks over Seel Lake.

During the first part of the 1920s, the main source of George's income was through trapping. His trapline was a long and narrow rectangle that started on the south side of the Tahtsa River opposite Sibola Creek and extended south to the Coast Mountains. In 1922, the BC government started registration of traplines. However, it was not until the late 1920s that most of the traplines were registered and marked on maps. George registered his trapline in the fall of 1930. The description states that the trapline goes "from a point about 1 mile [1.6 kilometres] south of Tahtsa River (Troitsa Pass) and about 2 miles [3.2 kilometres] NE of the confluence of Tahtsa River and Kasalka Creek in a south-westerly direction for about 15 miles [24 kilometres] to a point on Coles Lake about 1 mile NW of the outlet." George's trapline was in heavy timber that was mainly balsam. He had three cabins and two lean-tos along his line. The main cabin was on the Tahtsa River. The second was about 12 kilometres along his trapline near Lean-to Creek, and there was a cabin at Coles Lake. Later, the trapline was expanded to include all of the area around Coles Lake. George maintained his trapline throughout his lifetime, and, after his death, his son Rupert continued to use it. The main animal that George trapped was marten. Other fur-bearing animals that he caught included fisher, weasel, mink, wolverine, fox, coyote, muskrat and beaver. Throughout the 1920s the price for fur was fairly high, and the region had abundant wildlife. The trapline to the northwest was the territory of Baptiste Louie, while the trapline to the southwest initially belonged to Michel Edmond, a member of the Cheslatta First Nation, and later to G. S. Eddings.

In 1925, George became a Canadian citizen. His prospecting finally achieved results in the summer of 1926. There had been mining claims on the north side of the Tahtsa drainage on Mount Sweeney and the Sibola Range, but little mineral activity on the south side. Bill Sweeney had been one of the prospectors who had discovered and staked the Emerald Glacier mineral claims on the north side of the Tahtsa River in 1915. At his suggestion, George searched for a similar rock outcrop across the valley on the south side. On Swing Peak, about six kilometres from the Tahtsa River, he found and staked three claims that he named the Swannell Group. George made several trips down to the Tahtsa River, carrying ore that he sent to Trail so that its contents could be ascertained. The results showed the presence of silver and lead, with small amounts of zinc, copper and gold.

In early summer 1927, George was involved in a dramatic incident that was described in several newspapers. The initial account came from the Burns Lake *Observer* on July 7.

> **Wm. Grell loses life in rapids of Tahtsa River**
>
> **Rescue of other boat occupant was effected by George Seal [Seel] after weary wait for his arrival**
>
> **Victoria man marooned on marshy island for three days and nights**
>
> Wm. Grell of Ootsa Lake lost his life in the rapids of Tahtsa River on July 1st when his boat struck a log jam. The other occupant of the boat, J. H. Dawson of Victoria, was also precipitated into the water and coming up between two logs, managed to make his way to an adjoining island. He saw Grell make his way to the other shore and catch hold of a willow branch. Grell then turned and looked at him and immediately after was either seized with cramps or had heart failure for he released his hold on the willow and his body was seen tumbling over and over in the rapid stream.
>
> The island on which Dawson found himself was partially submerged with deep streams running through in many places. He knew that George Seal was expected to be up in the vicinity in the course of a few days and his problem was to try and intercept him. Meanwhile the river was rising and his position was becoming more untenable. There were a number of channels which Seal could take and Dawson spent his days in plunging through the heavy willow bottom, up to his waist in water in his endeavor to keep the various channels under observation. Though wet through from his plunging around the swamp and crossing the small channels, Mr. Dawson was able to get a little rest at night on a big log which just kept clear of the water. On the third day he heard George Seal's motor and was unable to get to the other side where the motor could be heard. Seal by some impulse took a channel through

> the submerged island—which he had never done before—and this brought him to the scene of the accident and to the rescue...
>
> When the accident occurred Grell and Dawson were returning from a trip up to the Whitesail to investigate mining properties there. Mr. Seal took Mr. Dawson to Ootsa Lake and on Monday Mr. Dawson arrived in Burns Lake apparently none the worse for his severe mental and physical strain.

In the fall of 1928, Grell's body was discovered and Stephen Hoskins, coroner and Government Agent from Smithers, conducted the coroner's inquiry. The inquiry, which provides information that is relevant to both "Shorty" Grell and the history of the Ootsa Lake area, is included in an appendix at the end of this book.

George needed financial backing to make a mine on Swing Peak a reality. In July 1927, he met a famous British Columbia boat captain who spent much of his wealth investing in mines. In an article on July 28, the Burns Lake *Observer* reported on the presence of Captain John Irving in the Ootsa Lake area.

> **Capt. Irving says steamboats feasible from White Sail to Ootsa Lake Landing**
>
> Returning from a trip to the head of the Tahtsa River Captain John Irving reports the river still in full flood, but with every indication of a rapid drop as the snow is nearly gone from the big hills.
>
> Years of experience in the swiftest rivers of British Columbia and Alaska entitle the Captain to speak with authority on the possibilities of operating light draft steamboat, which he states could be made quite feasible from the White Sail to Ootsa Lake landing with the expenditure of a few thousand dollars in blowing out log jams, and blocking some of the many side channels which take the water from the main channel.

Opposite: Frank Swannell took this picture of William (Shorty) Grell in 1922. Grell (known as Shorty Dunn at that time) was one of Bill Miner's accomplices in the famous BC train robbery near Kamloops. He received a life sentence but was paroled after eight years and eventually came to the Ootsa Lake area where he became a trapper and worked at Henson's store at Marilla. Frank Swannell photograph. Royal BC Museum, BC Archives I-58840

> Captain Irving visited several mining properties in the Lakes District, and is displaying great interest in George Seel's latest discovery of high grade silver-lead on the Tahtsa River some three miles above the spot where the late Billy Grell came to his death in one of the log jams, which should be removed.
>
> The captain was accompanied on his trip by G. S. Eddings of Ootsa Lake and Barney Mulvaney, and on the way up stream was lucky to pick up George Seel, whose knowledge of every crook and turn in the river was of inestimable value.

The Prince George *Citizen* also covered Irving's visit and noted:

> Captain John Irving, one of the pioneers of British Columbia, is taking another flier at mining... When he quit steamboating the captain went into mining, a venture in which he is said to have lost all the money he had.

Accompanying Irving was a veteran mining engineer, Charles Leslie Copp. Irving's trip coincided with a visit to the Tahtsa River area by the BC government's district mining engineer, Douglas Lay. Lay, who had not inspected the mining activity in this part of his district the previous year, wanted to view Seel's discovery. He also wanted to see the nearby Emerald Glacier mine where the Consolidated Mining and Smelting Company (today Teck Resources) had taken an option on the property and was getting ready to start developing it more extensively. There was also a new discovery near Whitesail Lake. Lay took photographs of Seel's mineral claims and these were included in the annual photograph album that the Department of Mines compiled. In the 1927 Department of Mines annual report, Lay made this notation in the New Discoveries section of his district: "Swannell group on Swing Peak mountain, south side Tahtsa River, Sibola section, Omineca mining division—a discovery of galena and zinc-blende containing good silver values, made last year by George Seel."

Lay also wrote a summary of Seel's mineral claims.

Swing Peak Mountain

This is a view of Swing Peak, where George Seel's mining claims were located, taken from the Tahtsa River. Bureau of Mines photograph album. Royal BC Museum, BC Archives J-00858

Swannell: This group of three claims, owned by George Seel of Wistaria, is situated on the northern slopes of Swing Peak mountain on the south side of the Tahtsa River. It is readily reached by motor-boat from Ootsa Lake post office, which is distant 40 miles [64 kilometres] by motor-road from Burns Lake, the nearest railway station on the Canadian National Railway. Seel Landing on the Tahtsa River at the foot of Swing Peak mountain (about a mile [1.6 kilometres] below Sweeney Landing) is distant about 63 miles [100 kilometres] from Ootsa Lake post office. A trail some 3 ½ miles [6 kilometres] in length leads from Seel Landing to the property.

At an elevation of 4,930 feet [1500 metres] there is exposed by open-cuts and natural agencies a shear-zone replacement fissure in the enclosing porphyritic volcanic rocks on the steeply sloping mountain side. Where fully exposed by open-cut the width of the fissure is 9 feet 6 inches [2.85 metres]. Mineralization is mainly confined to a width of 10 inches [25 centimetres] on the foot-wall and consists essentially of galena and zinc-blende, together with small amounts of chalcopyrite and grey copper. The fissure strikes S. 30°E. (magnetic), with steep, almost vertical, dip to the southwest. The fissure does not entirely coincide with the bedding planes of the enclosing country rock, which strike S. 40°E. (magnetic) and dip northeast. The mineral has a tendency in places to follow

Captain John Irving on Swing Peak near the mine site. Bureau of Mines photograph album. Royal BC Museum, BC Archives J-00857

A panorama of Swing Peak taken from about the same location in 2015. Photo Jay Sherwood

Captain John Irving, left, mining engineer C. L. Copp (centre) holding an ore sample, and George Seel in front of the mine entrance. Bureau of Mines photograph album. Royal BC Museum, BC Archives J-00859

along the bedding planes, apparently following small branch veins. It might be noted that this feature is exhibited by other shear-zones in the Sibola section. This shear-zone is exposed for a length of about 300 feet [90 metres] along its strike. Some very beautiful specimens of blood-red zinc-blende were observed. A sample of picked ore from the open-cut assayed: gold, trace; silver, 70 oz. [1984.5 grams] to the ton; lead 58 per cent; zinc, 5 per cent.

About 200 feet [60 metres] east of the above described fissure, at a lower elevation, is exposed by natural agencies, another shear-zone showing some nice clean galena and a little zinc-blende. This strikes S. 15°E. (magnetic) and dips northeast. These two fissures are likely to intersect higher up the mountain and quite possibly on the property other shear-zones exist which should be looked for. A sample of the last-mentioned shear-zone, of selected ore, assayed: gold, trace; silver, 162 oz. [4593 grams] to the ton; lead 40 per cent; zinc 8 per cent.

While very little development has been done on this property, appearances promise well. The surrounding geology is favourable and good silver values are a gratifying feature. The topography lends itself to economic exploration by drifts on the vein from the surface and the property clearly merits further development. It seems a reasonable expectation that such

George's mining claims on Swing Peak are still retained by his descendants; this photograph shows George's grandson at the mine site in 2015. Photo Jay Sherwood

development will disclose bodies of ore which can be hand sorted to good shipping grade. Before any underground work is started it is, however, recommended, as being a sound maxim applying to prospects generally, that the surface be thoroughly prospected first and that open-cuts be made at intervals in the fissures already discovered.

Noteworthy is the fact that the owner last year with commendable energy packed on his back several hundred pounds of ore from his property down to the Tahtsa River, conveyed it in his motor boat to Ootsa Lake post office, and shipped it to the smelter at Trail.

The property suffers from a certain geographic disability, in common with others in this section, but if developments warranted it, navigation on the Tahtsa River could be greatly improved by clearing out obstructions and log jams in the river channel and so facilitating shipments via Burns Lake. This property is commended to the attention of examining engineers.

The most momentous event for George in 1927 was his marriage, which took place in September. George was now in his late thirties, and with the prospect of financial success from his mining claims, he decided that he wanted to get married. In the fall of 1926, shortly after staking his mining claims, he placed advertisements in newspapers in Germany seeking a woman who wanted to come to live at Ootsa Lake and be his wife. The notice attracted the attention of Else Lübcke in Berlin.

Born in 1894 in Schivelbein, Pomerania (a region in northeast Germany that is part of Poland today), Else's father was an estate manager who died when she was young. During World War I, she moved to Berlin where she lived with her mother and aunt in an apartment. Beginning in 1924, she worked in the archives of a bank clipping newspaper articles and there saw George's advertisement. In Berlin, Else was part of the vibrant culture of the city, actively participating in the literary community and writing herself. She had short stories and poems published beginning in 1921. When she saw George's notice she was in her early thirties. The prospect of living indefinitely with her mother and aunt and working in a mundane job appeared oppressive to Else, while the opportunity to move to a romantic setting in Canada provided a chance to change her life. She responded to George's notice and they began exchanging letters and postcards. In a postcard to George on May 23, 1927 she asked George to "tell me exactly what papers I need for the marriage!" On June 18, she sent another postcard: "I just spent three days with your relatives. We had wonderful sunny weather! They were all very nice to me and send you their greetings! I took some photographs, helped with haymaking, and celebrated Corpus Christi. I will write in more detail as soon as I get home."

Else made the decision to leave Germany and go to Canada, with the intent of marrying George. In August she travelled by train to Hamburg where she boarded the *Empress of Australia*, one of the ships of the Canadian Pacific line. Else entered Canada at Quebec on August 27, where she listed her occupation as bank clerk, stated that she was a fiancée, and that she was going to George Seel in Wistaria. Else took a CPR train across the country, stopping for a brief visit in Winnipeg. On the journey across Canada she reflected on her decision to spend her life with someone she had never seen before: "You see, princess on the pea, now you get King Thrushbeard since no one was good enough for you." She also wrote that she was having trouble sleeping because she was both anxious and excited, and wondering what she was getting into. On September 5 she arrived in Vancouver and by arrangement checked into the St. Francis Hotel at the corner of Cordova and Seymour streets near the train station.

There she met George. She wrote, "I arrived, saw Georg and calmed down. I am very happy and hope that everything will be alright. A few letters in a newspaper brought me luck. Yes, who dares, wins. Georg is a good and real man; that is the best thing possible." She described their initial meeting: "There is a knock on the door. Georg comes in, he is shy, sheepish, tall, with broad shoulders and strong hands. We both cannot speak, we stutter, finally I laugh and then it is easier. Five minutes later we go out. I buy three ties for him—he only has one, a terrible blue thing and only two handkerchiefs. He has worn the tie for three years and I said: 'I hope you have not worn your shirt that long!' " The next day they got married. Else described the day in her diary.

> Today is my wedding day. I think about all the literature on this, the fairy-tale like ideas we have with a wreath and veil and banns six weeks in advance and a feast with all aunts and relatives, and I have to laugh. How good do I feel at this moment; how happy.
>
> This morning we didn't even know if we wanted to get married. Then the old Captain Irving came, Georg told him something and then we were standing in the courthouse before the sheriff and Georg had to vow that it was his holy will to marry me and to treat me well. Then we had the five dollar licence in our pocket and went to Miss Watson who quickly drove us in her own car to the Reverend of the United Church of Canada. He had appeared in a smart travel suit, had blond hair, and wrote down everything slowly and carefully. Georg didn't know his mother's maiden name and I didn't know the birth place of my father. It was easy in Germany. However, it didn't matter and the Reverend gave a little speech on the sunshine of love and a happy life and also a bit about Christ and the Holy Spirit. Georg pulled out a ring that he had bought half an hour earlier. Even the Reverend in his travel suit kissed me and I was Mrs. Seel. Now I am married.
>
> Later we had a beer with Captain Irving, walked hand in hand down to the harbour, bought a sweater, pajamas and a wrist watch for Georg, and for me a fountain pen and also half a pound of chocolates. We were happy as larks and now I am in our room and 'my husband' went for dinner and I write those great events in my diary. I am convinced that Georg and I will have a happy marriage.

George was anxious to return to Wistaria. Else wrote, "We stayed in Vancouver only for two more days... Our steamer left at 7 pm... and the old Captain came to say good bye. He kissed my hand and disappeared and Georg came up to me."

They travelled by boat to Prince Rupert.

> I would have liked to stay for a day but Georg wanted to go home. We mounted the train that was already waiting. Many cars were full of happy, singing and chatting Indians. The night passed while I was lying in Georg's lap but I couldn't sleep. The next day, on Sunday, around noon we arrived in Burns Lake. Barney Mulvaney, a burly blond man in his mid-fifties, greeted us and took us to Ruddy's Hotel [the Cheslatta]...
>
> On Monday we travelled with Norman Schreiber, also of German descent. Forest on both sides and the big François Lake. There was actually a real, good ferry. We went to the other shore and we were greeted by Mrs. Schreiber, dressed like an amazon in breeches and jockey cap...
>
> We went to the post office and stayed overnight in Mrs. Schreiber's house. The next morning Georg went ahead in his motor boat. We waited until 11 a.m.... Then we left for Wistaria. I kept on asking Mrs. Schreiber "Is this Wistaria?" whenever I saw a log cabin. Finally, around 1 p.m. we stopped at the post office in Wistaria. A small hut with a separate sleeping area for the family. Friendly people who offered me food, and finally Georg.
>
> After a short visit with our neighbour, a farmer who had come 5 years ago from Ireland, I insisted to go home and we went down to the boat. The boat went further and further along the Ootsa Lake. "Where is our house?" I asked. "Not yet." "Where is our house?" I shouted. "Not yet." Only the shore and trees, and more shore and more trees. And suddenly I realized: loneliness. When you scream, nobody will hear you. It felt like a stab in the heart. Then a pretty little wooden house appeared.
>
> I couldn't see it clearly through the tears in my eyes. I was going to move into my own home in Wistaria, B.C. in Canada, on September 13, 1927.

George remained home for a month and did a lot of work around the house. In her diary Else wrote on October 16: "In my new home! I am here for a month already and still very happy. Georg went to the mountains three days

Else took this photograph of Grace Schreiber, who was a schoolteacher at Ootsa Lake until she married Norman Schreiber. University of Victoria Archives 4-3-08

ago to set up traps." She felt sorry for the animals being killed for their fur but knew this was part of George's livelihood, and they planned to use the money he earned to buy furniture and send some funds to their mothers.

November 9 was her birthday and she noted that she didn't see anybody all day. "Am I sad? No. I got used to this; I read and write and have enough company. When I get up in the morning it is cold. I light a fire and get water. My little dog and my cat follow me curiously."

She commented on the people around her. "The next neighbour is 'Old Bill' [Harrison] who fathered a dozen children and plays the violin beautifully... Currently, only the second son, Cliff, lives at home, together with his young wife and their baby." She noted that one of his sons, Ed Harrison, lived on the other side.

Else reflected on George and her situation.

> I really love Georg. He is so good, calm and strong. He is like the landscape; he is a part of it and when he spent months and years hunting alone in the mountains; discovering lakes one of which even bears his name... How well he can do everything, how skilled he is; he understands everything and I admire him.

Home at Wistaria. Else Seel photograph. University of Victoria Archives 4-6-19

> When we hung up the first laundry we stood at the window and saw it flutter in the sunshine. Georg put his arms around me and said in an almost solemn manner: "As long as the Earth exists this is the first time that laundry is being dried here." For the first time!
>
> I think this is what I find so compelling here: everything for the first time.

By the time she penned her next diary entry on November 18, George had been away for over a month and she wrote about her feelings.

> Every day now I don't do anything except waiting. Waiting that Georg comes back from hunting in the mountains. It seems that he is actually a fisherman and not a hunter since I always look out onto the water, listening for the quick, bright "tak-tak-tak" sound of the boat engine. Around 5 pm, when it starts to get dark, I huddle up on the biggest chair; the freezing cold comes in through the cracks in the floor and my feet get icy cold. I look at the mountains and the sky; snow clouds drift along sullenly, looking for a place where they can let go of their load. The sun doesn't have a lot of strength; it is a milky-white

Cliff Harrison (left) and George outside the Seel house. Else Seel photograph. University of Victoria Archives 4-3-14

> behind the dusky darkness. For how long will I sit by this window? Actually, my whole life—but this is impossible. It is like I am pumping my body up with light and strength to fly away. And still, I know this stupid world so well. Why am I then so restless? Here is the better part of the day, of life—long icicles hang down low in front of the window. I shoveled a path through the snow from the house to the lake. The air is so fresh and clear that I can almost taste it.
>
> Yes, I have a good life here, but it seems that I don't have a husband. After Christmas Georg will stay home, thank God. Every day now I don't do anything except waiting.

She wrote about being by herself.

> At first I was scared to be alone. Listened to the little wolves [coyotes] howling. Now I am much calmer. Not even a month ago I would run over to Old Bill when the Indians went to the mountains and their fires were burning right across the lake. I thought they might come over here any minute, set our house on fire, and would tie me to the stake.

By November 27 George's planned return date had passed. "Georg has been away one week longer than he said. Day and night during this long week I thought to hear him coming every moment, by boat or on foot. But there was nothing." She used the time to write her first article from Wistaria. It was about her journey to Ootsa Lake and she was sending it to the women's magazine *Frau und Gegenwart* (*Women and the Present*). She hoped that it would be accepted and that she would receive some money to send to her mother.

One other important event occurred for George in 1927. His claims became part of a mining company, and the information was posted in the *British Columbia Gazette* on November 10, 1927.

> **Certificate of Incorporation No. 9757.**
>
> I hereby certify that "Tahtsa Mining Company, Limited (Non-Personal Liability)" has this day been incorporated under the "Companies Act" as a Specially Limited Company. The capital of the Company is two hundred and fifty thousand dollars, divided into two hundred and fifty thousand shares. The registered office of the Company is situate at Vancouver, in the Province of British Columbia. Given under my hand and seal of office at Victoria, Province of British Columbia, this fifth day of November, one thousand nine hundred and twenty-seven. H. G. Garrett, Registrar of Companies.

This would enable George and the people who were promoting the mine to get financial backing to try to develop the claims into a viable mine.

George returned in mid-December with some furs that he trapped. He and Else went to the trading post at Ootsa Landing, about thirty kilometres away, where the proprietor, Norm Schreiber, bought the furs. They stayed overnight, and since Norm's wife was out of town, he let them use their bedroom. Else wrote: "We slept in the Schreiber's double bed, which I thought was quite funny. The pouring rain thawed the snow and around midnight—splash—came a gush of water through the thin ceiling, and we woke with a start. Georg got a tub and the water was dripping noisily all night, and the full moon shone happily through the small window."

George and Else returned to Wistaria by boat, travelling with Charlie Lindquist, a Swedish trapper: "It was cold and the lake covered with a thin layer of ice, but it was a wonderful trip. Charlie and I and Lumpel, my dog, under a down blanket, and Georg at the engine." On the trip, they stopped and had a meal with one of the families who lived along the lake.

> Andersons are the only ones around here who have a piano, and I asked Mrs. Anderson to play me a Beethoven piece. She played the Moonlight Sonata really well; I was surprised and pleased. She also played the Peer Gynt Suite that I had heard often, and now here, "Far from Madrid." Never had I listened so intently! Then the two women [Mrs. Anderson and a neighbour, Mrs. McNeil] sang English duets. Mrs. McNeill with her low alto voice sang particularly well. It was a real little afternoon of music here in Wistaria, B.C.
>
> Towards evening we came home and quickly lit a fire. Charlie was our first guest. He slept on the floor with his eiderdown blanket.

Else described Christmas at Wistaria:

> There was pig slaughtering at Cummins, then a Christmas tree dance at the [community] hall. Presents for the children were hanging on the Christmas tree. After some singing and reciting the children got their presents, then there were sweets and lots of dancing. I was continuously asked to dance and met Walter Bär, a Swiss German. The "ch" sound that I knew from Switzerland sounded so nice... My Christmas tree was decorated with

George cutting firewood. Else Seel photograph. University of Victoria Archives 3-31-7

> candles. The children liked it, and had fun blowing them out. Later I set up a few little things, without the usual ceremonies though. Georg said that he couldn't get excited about it, but that is not important I think. I am very happy though—especially when it comes to unwrapping presents!

In early January, George left for the trapline. Else wrote on January 5:

> The new year began with −45°F [-42°C]. I didn't see anyone; they all stayed home by the fire. My breath froze on the quilt and Georg had lumps of ice on his moustache—in bed. Now he is gone again, after he had been here for a good three weeks. Yes, a good three weeks—as good as he is himself, steady and calm, made for the eternity of marriage. But, it still seems to me like I am unmarried.

She stated that while George was home he "was really kind-hearted. He got up first in the morning and made himself breakfast. He is very good to me. But will he always be like this? Nobody is."

Else reflected on her changing moods: "Earlier today I danced by myself in the house because I felt so happy and light, but now I have a heavy heart because I know that it is all up to me—married, marriage: words like mountains; they either crush you or you climb over them into the light."

On the way to the post office. Else Seel photograph. University of Victoria Archives 4-3-14

Else learned to handle the cold, snow and long winters. Twice a week she walked three kilometres to the post office to get mail and meet other people. Else had subscriptions to some magazines and ordered library books on loan, so there was often reading material for her in the mail. There was water to be hauled from the lake, wood to be brought in, housework, letters and articles to write, along with books and magazines to read. She also participated in community events and gradually got to know some of the people who lived in the area around her. In one of her diary entries that winter she wrote: "At night I still dream of Berlin and old friends, but when I wake up and look out of the window and see the snow-covered hills, the unending forest and the mountains, I take a deep breath and thank God."

After her diary entry in early January, Else did not write again until February 18.

> Time goes by. It is only now, when I see the sun set behind the mountains every afternoon, that I truly understand those words. It is different every day; sometimes yellow-golden bays, sometimes milky veils, then a rust-red disk in a completely clear sky, and yesterday a fiery oven that made my heart beat and my feet dance. I stomped my feet and sang sounds that came to me, felt like I was obsessed and kept facing the sun. I spun around with stretched-out arms like in a ritual dance, shouting and jubilating, because I knew: you are alone—completely alone. Nobody can hear you, nobody can see you.

Else noted that "Georg is gone again for a week. Last time he had caught only 4 marten, just enough to pay for food." She also described attending a concert at the school in Streatham.

> Cliff H[arrison] picked us up. The horses were up to their stomach in the snow and we made slow progress. We were three families in the big sleigh. The two babies took turns in crying, sitting on their mothers' laps. The women chatted "gak-gak-gak," very fast so that I couldn't understand them... The trees with their heavy white pelt caps looked grotesque: they looked like jumping dogs, old men or scarecrows. It was a beautiful ride. The program was a variety show of singing and dancing involving the schoolchildren and some adults and was well-attended by settlers from around the area.

Finally, she noted that she had a visit from Jimmy Andrews. Andrews, a Wet'suwet'en First Nation man, lived at the west end of Ootsa Lake at a place now called Andrews Bay. He was an occasional visitor to the Seel residence through the years.

In her diary entry for March 6, Else commented on George's absence: "Today it's exactly 3 weeks that Georg is away. During the first week I think: maybe it's good that we have to be apart sometimes, it keeps the love fresh. During the second week I look at the calendar and think 'how much longer'. During the third week I get a bit lonely and wish that he would be coming back soon. And during the fourth week I look out the window if I can see him when he appears at the end of the lake."

She wrote about a priest whom she met at the Wistaria post office who wanted to visit one of the Harrison family members: "The priest also talked about Aristotle and tried to explain his teachings and principles; then the horses pulled him through the deep snow, I showed him the path down to the lake, to the neighbours. This was the first visitor from the old world and its 'culture': a priest who is teaching 'savages' who are already—according to Seume—better people." (Johann Gottfried Seume was a German writer of the late eighteenth and early nineteenth century who spent time in Nova Scotia in the 1780s and met some Mi'kmaq people. He wrote a poem called *Der Wilde* (*The Savage*) which presented a sympathetic view of a First Nations person who provided life-saving assistance to a settler who had mistreated him. Some people considered Seume's writings about Canada to be the beginning of German-Canadian writing.)

A few days later Else wrote about baking bread for the first time. This was a special experience for her, since she did not do much cooking in Germany, and she was proud that she managed to make her own bread. She also talked about the freedom of being by herself: "I played with Lumpel [the dog] and all of a sudden I started singing. It was like being drunk and I had that wonderful feeling that there was no apartment building, no street, barely any paths and

Opposite: Jimmy Andrews, a member of the Wet'suwet'en First Nation, was born and raised at the western end of Ootsa Lake in the area now called Andrews Bay. Andrews was a trapper who also worked for some of the local guides. He was respected and well liked by the people of Wistaria. In the 1930s, Andrews built a cabin on Harrison property near the Seel residence so that his children could attend the school at Wistaria. This arrangement boosted school enrollment and prevented Andrews' children from attending residential school. Jimmy Andrews and his family frequently visited the Seel residence. Else Seel photograph. University of Victoria Archives 4-6-27

no people. I am singing and I am singing sometimes out of tune and jump around in a silly and childish manner; the animals don't care."

In her entry for March 19, Else noted the first signs of spring. She was sitting in front of her house with the cat and dog, and despite George's absence she was happy. She wrote, "Today Georg has been away in the mountains for five weeks. All of last week I was waiting for him. I baked cake, made soup etc. but didn't eat a lot myself and lost weight. But my mind is very alert again and I have to feed it again." She noted that "Yesterday, on Sunday, I went to the post office as usual, and as always enchanted by this wonderful piece of the Earth. All of a sudden, by the ditch where I crossed the bridge, I looked up and shouted, 'Pussy willows!' Yes, silvery and most charmingly they were swinging above me. On the way back, Mr. Cummins cut off a few branches for me. I cradled them affectionately in my arms. My pussy willows!"

Else wrote in her diary for March 30 that George had returned, but only for five days. She did a lot of cooking and baking because George didn't have a lot of food when he was away, writing that "I wanted Georg to eat as much as he wanted during his few days off. When he was away in the mountains he had so little food that one day he even had to make do with a marten!" He brought lots of good furs, but she felt sorry for the animals. She wondered whether she felt sorry for rats, but she liked it when she heard the pack rats between the walls in the house at night because the noise made her feel not so alone. Norman Schreiber bought the pelts for two hundred dollars. Else kept the darkest marten to sell at the fur auction in Vancouver.

Else enjoyed the visitors that came:

"While Georg was home, Charlie Lindquist and Jack Cain came for dinner and stayed overnight. I was really happy that from now on I would always have such visitors, all real men who didn't care a bit about regulations through and through... The next morning all three of them left again. Charlie and Jack went back home and Georg back into the mountains."

George finished his trapping by mid-April. On April 22 she wrote:

> Today is Sunday and post office day! Just now Georg went to get the mail. He has been here for three days now and will stay home for two months. How wonderful is that! This morning we sowed cabbage; green cabbage and cauliflower, putting two seeds in each little hole. For now the box will stay by the window and end of May the little seedlings will be put in the ground outside. This first sowing felt odd, as if the seed had been dropped inside me too, as if something was growing inside me. All this unknown makes me shiver and at the same

> time I feel a sweet lust and everything sinks: the little fame and the little ambition; a force glows in me. Oh summer in this holy land, come quickly.
>
> The rooster crowed and keeps an eye on things. He calls the hens when he finds a nice morsel of food. Georg brings me toast and coffee in bed each morning; I lie there, listen to the outside and inside and feel the blood rushing through my body—infinite happiness. The sun shines when I get up and work is done quickly and easily. How extraordinary lucky I am!

At the beginning of May, they cleared land for a garden and planted black, red and white currants, gooseberry bushes, horseradish, rhubarb, strawberries, asparagus, potatoes, onions and other vegetables. Else wrote how watching swans flying reinforced her connection with the life she was living at Wistaria.

> Yesterday 4 flocks of wild swans flew over Ootsa Lake towards the mountains. They cried like our tame, fat birds at home but they flew incredibly high and were barely visible. How amazing those animals are in the wild and how clumsy they are at home on the farm where they have trouble waddling over a piece of wood. It's always the same how being locked up spoils everything that's strong, happy and fresh. When I wake up in the morning I see, like from a long distance, thousands of people in Berlin trudging to work, day in and day out, and I was one of them for a decade. Now I have lost this unnatural patience and conformability and could never again participate in such a dull and listless manner. I want to stay, live and die here.

In an article on May 10, the Burns Lake *Observer* reported on the Tahtsa Mining Company and their plans for the upcoming year.

> **Quarter Million Dollars for Tahtsa Development Work**
>
> The Tahtsa Mining Co. with an authorized capital of $250,000.00 is preparing for a big season of development work on the properties discovered by George Seel, the well-known trapper and prospector formerly of Burns Lake, but now firmly established as a farmer in the Wistaria district.
>
> The mineral claims are located in the Cibola district of the Omineca Mining Division on Swing Peak Mountain within a few miles of the Sweeney Mountain and Cibola discoveries.

According to such authorities as Dr. J. F. Marshall, Dominion Government geologist, Dr. V. F. Dolmage of the same department, and Dr. C. O. Swanson, Professor of Geology University of Wisconsin, the higher values in silver-lead ores are carried by tetrahedrite and freibergite. Although the existence of these ores was presumed by these mineralogists, the actual discovery was made by George Seel in his finding the argentiferous galena with high values in silver and lead with grey copper, the width of the main vein being nine and a half feet.

Five samples taken across this vein by Captain John Irving and Barney Mulvaney ran as follows:

Sample no.	Gold	Silver	Copper	Zinc	Lead
1	Trace	108			
2	0.06	168		10	46
3	Trace	133	4.5	6	52
4	Trace	150			60
5	Trace	235	4.0	5	62

William Dawson, who also examined the property after Captain Irving, reported that he was highly pleased with it and reported assays running as high as 2000 ozs. [56,700g] of silver.

In his agreement with the Tahtsa Mining Company, George Seel insisted on continuous work being done on the claims, which are known as the Swannell group, named in honor of the government engineer of that name...

Captain John Irving, the sole promoter of the enterprise, is well and widely known in British Columbia as a solver of difficult transportation problems, and considers the shipping of ores from the Cibola, Tahtsa and Whitesail an easy matter. Boat materials and machinery are on the way and Bill Sweeney is taking in a gang to shoot the tips off the most dangerous sweepers in forty miles of river—pending the awakening of the

> Department at Ottawa to the needs of an adequate appropriation in order to make the Tahtsa River navigable even to such men as Johnny Irving...

George didn't stay the full two months as planned. Else wrote in her diary on May 22: "On Sunday morning Georg went with Mr. Sweeney and Charlie Lindquist by boat to the mountains to clean out the Tahtsa River and I will be alone again for two weeks." Since both the Emerald Glacier and Tahtsa Mining Company planned on working their claims in the summer, they needed to blast the log-jams out of the Tahtsa River to make it easier and safer for boats to navigate the waterway. In addition to the dynamite, the men also took some provisions for the men working at the mine sites during the summer.

Else noted: "The lake is open, the wind blows from the mountains, the water was roaring and foaming like back then the Baltic Sea in Kolbergermünde, where I used to listen and wishing myself far, far away."

Bill Sweeney (left), Charlie Lindquist (centre) and George leaving for Tahtsa River in May 1928. Lindquist was a trapper in the Whitesail/Eutsuk Lake area for many years. A peak, lake and pass in the area are named for him. Else Seel photograph. University of Victoria Archives 4-4-05

She described an overnight trip that she took and for the first time wrote about being pregnant.

> I was away, even if it was only for two days in Ootsa Lake. The weather was warm and sunny, the ice cracked and broke like glass and clinked like wine glasses: Cheers! Ootsa Lake! I walked along the shore for hours. Giant trees stood by the water and the first green climbed up the hill. Along the path stood cabin after cabin and the first church on Ootsa Lake. It was a tiny building with a small window through which I looked curiously. Inside were rows of seats, the benches, but the door hung in its hinges, askew and abandoned. The first Indian huts, also dead and empty, since the Indians love the outdoors. They are out now fishing, and hunting beavers. Georg met them and the wife of the chief Baptiste gave him two beaver teeth as a present for me. The Indians wear those as bracelets.
>
> Later I got to Mrs. van Tyne's hut. She quickly came out, wearing a red dress, looking fresh and friendly. The children's laundry fluttered and I saw the single big room where bed stood beside bed. Only the three youngest ones crawled around, the other six were at school. And still, everything was clean and fresh. Nine children, I don't understand it. I keep on thinking what I will do with the one that I carry under my heart. Mrs. van Tyne led me to Skin Tyee's old campground; there was nothing except a few fallen trees and bushes and an old rack for drying fish that consisted of a few parallel branches between bushes. This is where the old, wild chief who hated white people had lived for a quarter of a century.

That evening Else stayed at the Bennett Hotel at Ootsa Lake. While she was there, Barney Mulvaney, a prominent resident of Burns Lake arrived with a Liberal politician and Bill Sweeney. The next day Else drove with the three men to Wistaria. She recorded that "In the evening we got to our little house and Georg came out, surprised to see his wife getting out of a car with three gentlemen. Then I turned immediately into a busy housewife, making supper... My weekend away from pots and pans, from making the beds, cleaning and washing dishes was over." Sweeney stayed overnight, the first person to use their new guest room in the attic.

On May 29, she wrote in her diary: "Out of 9 months of marriage I have been alone for 7 months. Sometimes I don't see anybody for days. And still I am very happy and not so alone; always in the best company."

Grave for a son of Skin Tyee. Else Seel photograph. University of Victoria Archives 4-3-09

At the beginning of July, Else went to visit the nearest doctor, who was at Burns Lake, regarding her pregnancy. She was there during Dominion Day where they had a Wild West Show, which she thought quite tame, and pillow fighting and a log-rolling contest. A thunderstorm halted the activities. While she was in the community, she visited Mrs. Minnie Schjelderup. Her husband, Vilhelm, was a surveyor in Burns Lake, and he had articled to be a surveyor with Frank Swannell.

> We got to Mrs. Schjelderup's, a real, tasteful, pleasant home with modern English literature magazines and such. We had tea and Norwegian bread, and in the evening we went to a dance. It was overcrowded and I got kicked and pushed the whole time. I felt odd in the arms of strangers that held me tight, even though I was carrying a child inside me, and the strangers, the dance and the air made me sick. And still, all the women participated, and I was wondering how many would have been in the same condition.
>
> In the morning we went to Ruddy's Hotel where I had a room, and slept.

Else wanted to see Prince Rupert and more of the Pacific coast, so from Burns Lake she went on a sightseeing trip. She took the train to Prince Rupert, and there boarded the Canadian National Steamship Company's S.S. *Prince Charles* for a four-day trip. The ship travelled up the coast north of Prince Rupert, going to the head of Portland Canal, where it stopped at the mining community of Stewart. Else and a woman that she met on the ship walked over to Hyder, Alaska. The *Prince Charles* then went to Anyox, on Observatory Inlet. There was a large copper mine and smelter there, and Else observed that the trees and grass had been killed (the result of acid rain). The steamship then travelled to Queen Charlotte Islands (Haida Gwaii) and spent a day stopping at several ports before returning to Prince Rupert. Else returned to Ootsa in mid-July where they were having a picnic, followed the next day by the provincial election, held in hot weather, both events described in her diary:

> All kinds of games took place at the picnic in Ootsa Lake: pillow fighting, sack races, relays, shooting matches for a fat goose and an interesting baseball game between Burns Lake and Ootsa Lake, with Ootsa Lake the winner...

Else fishing at one of the small lakes on the benchland above Ootsa Lake in June 1928. University of Victoria Archives 4-4-05

The next day we went to the community hall to vote. Here, where [Arthur] Shelford the Conservative candidate resides, most people of course vote Conservative. Only 13 Liberal votes that they counted on one hand before. Nevertheless [Alexander] Manson succeeded in the district, even though the provincial government became Conservative this time, the first time in 12 years. [Alexander Manson was first elected as MLA for the Omineca riding in 1916 and was a Cabinet minister in the Liberal government in the 1920s. In 1928 he was elected for his fourth term. He won a fifth term in 1932, again defeating Shelford. Arthur's nephew, Cyril, became the MLA from Omineca for many years after World War II.]

My back got stiffer and stiffer and I could barely walk. During the night I got a fever and had a real flu the next day. I probably got it at the Keefe's. Their kids just recovered from it but I had slept in the bed of their eldest daughter when I stayed there overnight. Georg looked after me lovingly but Sweeney wanted to leave. So they went to Ootsa Lake to do their shopping and I thought to myself "they go to the mountains anyway, even when I am sick." But Georg waited one more day. He massaged me until I perspired and now I am still weak and in bed

A view of Prince Rupert and the harbour. Else Seel photograph. University of Victoria Archives 4-4-10

> while I hear the small engine outside. The boat left and I was alone again for weeks.

George was only gone for a couple of weeks, getting ready for the mine development. Then he returned to Wistaria to await the arrival of the mining engineer.

In her diary for August 14, Else mentioned his arrival: "Last week the mining engineer, Mr. Copp, came from Vancouver. I noticed how happy Georg was that things were finally shaping up and I was as excited as on my first day of school. Two days before we had finished the guest room... Then the boat left again."

Else noted that Copp stayed overnight with them. They had just painted the guest room where he slept and he didn't use the washing basin but washed in the lake. After Copp and George left, Else cleaned the house and went to the post office to get the mail, saying that "I always get letters, post cards, newspapers and magazines which helps with the loneliness." She also commented that it had been almost one year since she had left Berlin.

Totem pole on Haida Gwaii.
Else Seel photograph. University of Victoria Archives 4-4-11

On September 6 she recorded that she had been married for one year. She was also feeling her pregnancy more, and starting to be impatient for the baby to be born. George was not there to celebrate their anniversary, having left two days earlier: "He is taking provisions to his hunting cabins. For three weeks now we are waiting for money or a telegram from the old Captain. I don't understand what his ideas are with the mine. If nothing happens by the 27th of the month it will go back to Georg and we can try our luck again."

Else wrote about good news for the mine in her diary entry for September 20: "Yesterday, in storm and rain, Georg left for the mine with Mr. Copp and three other men. Even if it is late, at least they are starting. This happened mainly because of the initiative of Mr. Copp, who encouraged three of his managers to invest some money. In total they invest $15,000: 2000 right now for the start and the remaining 13,000 next spring. Now it all depends on how the mine turns out; good, I hope."

She also noted the arrival of fall: "There are waves on Ootsa Lake, the wind howls and shakes the yellow and colourful leaves and makes them fly around. Tomatoes and beans froze a while ago already. The cabbages are firm and magnificent."

Else wrote about several items in her diary entry for October 1.

> Rain and wind! Except for the four trees in front of the house, the loyal watchmen, almost all trees have lost their leaves.
>
> Again I am alone for two weeks! The child rolls around inside my body like a small globe, rebelling. The little planet wants to turn in space independent of me. Then the sun comes out for a few minutes like just now, making everything feel lighter and happier, and even the lake is smooth and well-behaved for a few moments.
>
> With the most recent mail came my article in the "Voss" [*Vossische Zeitung*]. It had a big headline, almost like an advertisement: "There are Germans everywhere"; meanwhile I had given it the much more modest title "An Outing to the Pacific."
>
> Well, the prophet is now far enough away from the home country and that alone makes him "entitled to big print." Now I cannot write enough! But I don't

Stewart. Else Seel photograph. University of Victoria Archives 4-4-12

> even think of it. Only what comes to my mind—no more and no less, and only what I feel like, and nothing commercial!

For her October 10 diary entry she noted that "Two days ago, when I woke up, the first snow was falling. Later the sun came out and took it away again. Winter will be here soon though!" She commented that the *Vossische Zeitung* sent her twelve dollars for her article "which I thought was rather paltry since it filled an entire page in their paper. Alas, I am far away from it all, and I know this all too well."

On November 1, Else wrote that she had gone to visit the doctor in Burns Lake and found out that he was getting ready to leave the community. She then decided that she would go to Hazelton for the birth of her child. Else was in her mid-thirties; this was her first child; and Dr. Wrinch and the hospital at Hazelton had a good reputation. While she was in Burns Lake, she visited Mrs. Schjelderup again. After staying at a hotel in Burns Lake, she returned to Ootsa Lake the next day with Norman Schreiber. She remained overnight with the Schreibers before returning home. She also commented: "Now the mine is closed. Mr. Copp wrote big cheques and Georg gave one to me. Laundry, visitors, making Sauerkraut etc. Barely one week and Georg was gone again, hunting. He left on Monday morning."

In the November 1 edition of the Burns Lake *Observer*, the newspaper described the activity of the Tahtsa Mining Company during 1928, and its plans for the following year.

> **Big Development next year on Seel Property at Tahtsa**
>
> **Mining expert says rich ore will bear all costs of transportation and leave big working margin.**
>
> **Cabins erected and trail is built**
>
> C. L. Copp, of Vancouver, acting on behalf of strong financial mining men, has taken over the Swannell Group on the Tahtsa and cabins have been erected and a good trail has been cut to the property. As soon as snow goes in the spring considerable money will be spent on development work.
>
> Mr. Copp personally recommends this property and states his opinion that the very high grade ore will stand the expense of transportation over the long trail to the railway of Burns Lake.
>
> Mr. Copp is one of the pioneering mining men of British Columbia and he carries great weight with local and foreign financiers.

Douglas Lay wrote a brief summary of the Tahtsa Mining Company's activities for the Department of Mines annual report, and took a photograph.

> Swannell. "A company has been incorporated to operate this property—namely, the Tahtsa Mining Company, Limited: the registered office is 510 Hastings Street West, Vancouver. During the year the company constructed camp buildings at the Tahtsa River and also close to the showings, this work being carried out under the direction of C. L. Copp. [The company's office was in the Standard Building, which still exists today.]

On November 14, Copp wrote to George from Vancouver:

> I am enclosing cheque for $100.00 and option to be signed, dated and witnessed, also a form of proxy so that I can represent you at the next general meeting. I made inquiries and I find that under the Companies Act it is necessary to hold a shareholders meeting once a year, so it will be necessary to send out notices very soon.
>
> The samples I brought with me ran 99.2 oz silver, 48 per cent lead, taken from last open cut up the hill. Our men are at Calgary, the Turner Valley oil excitement has got them all going here, there has been as much as a million dollars changing hands here on the stock exchange, mostly oil stock. I am looking for them back at the end of the present week.
>
> Capt. Irving and Miss Watson wish to be remembered to you and Mrs. Seel.

The packhorse is loaded with supplies to transport to the mine site. The cabin is the Copp cabin, built along the Tahtsa River at the beginning of the trail to the mine. It was located about five kilometres upstream from George's main trapping cabin. The Copp cabin remained along the Tahtsa for many years. University of Victoria Archives 4-6-33

A view of the building for the workers of the Tahtsa Mining Company. Bureau of Mines photograph album. Royal BC Museum, BC Archives J-00863

Constructing the bunkhouse for the workers of the Tahtsa Mining Company. University of Victoria Archives 4-6-33

Else wrote from François Lake on November 24.

> One week ago Georg came back in the wind and weather. At first I didn't hear the boat at all. Then here was my dear husband getting out of the boat with his rubber boots. He was very nice and brought me coffee and toast in the morning and the next evening I said goodbye to Mrs. Buster Harrison and Mrs. Cliff Harrison and they wished me good luck. The next day, Sunday at noon, in the sunshine we left. From the water our little house looked so pretty and small, and I wish to come back and continue to live there happily. We visited Cummins and Barkers on the fur farm. He showed us a magnificent, large silver fox that was three quarters silver. She told me horrific stories about difficult births where everything was full of blood. It made me feel ill and I could barely eat the cake that she served. In the evening we got to the Schreiber's and the night was gentle and sweet.

The next morning Else travelled with Norman Schreiber, who was going to Burns Lake. She wanted to cross François Lake on the ferry before it froze.

Henkel's lodge at François Lake. Else Seel photograph. University of Victoria Archives 4-4-06

She wrote that "At noon we were already in François Lake, by ferry and up the hill to the biggest and most beautiful wooden house in the whole area: François Lake Lodge." The proprietor of the lodge, Mrs. Johanna Henkel, was from Germany and Else planned to stay there until shortly before the birth of her child, who was due around Christmas.

On December 10, she wrote in her diary:

> I will be here only for another week and then go to Hazelton. I will be glad to leave. It feels too much like old people's lives here, interspersed with Strindberg's "Dance of Death." Does life always have to be like that in its second half? Heaven save me from such a stale broth; let me live and be full of life until the last moment or rather be dead.
>
> Yesterday I was in pain. The child kicked and kicked, and my poor body really hurt. I thought of Georg and how rarely he is with me, and how I am always so alone. It often feels like we barely know each other and now I am already having his child. It's unfathomable.

Four days later she noted: "Georg is coming tomorrow, and the day after tomorrow we will go to the hospital in Hazelton." From Hazelton she wrote on December 18:

> The doctor said that the baby would come in a week, everything good and normal. Georg and I went for a walk, up the mountain, the "town" below us. High up the mountain we came to an Indian graveyard with many little wooden houses with tiny doors and windows for the souls of the deceased, laden with presents and boxes and guns and even a sewing machine. And also, chiseled from stone, a dog's head, a bear, a frog, a monkey, a fox, and a duck. A squirrel ran quickly along the fence; Georg was good and loving as always. We saw the trail that leads to the Yukon telegraph line. I felt a desire to travel along it with a pack horse.
>
> Then came old Dr. Wrinch who interrupted our good-bye. I cried this time and didn't feel embarrassed. Georg was firm. I waved at him from the large porch with the carved roof, then he was gone.

The cemetery at Old Hazelton. Else Seel photograph. University of Victoria Archives 3-31-26

Else and George's first child, a son named Rupert, was born on December 22 at 6:00 am. Else described Christmas at the hospital.

> At 5 a.m. there was a stocking hanging on the wall saying "Rupert's first Christmas." A small soap Buddha with blue earrings and stamped "Paris" peered out from the top of the stocking and underneath were a baby jacket and coloured marbles, that I had once so much enjoyed myself...
>
> Santa Claus himself came in the afternoon, with a red and white coat, long beard and a mask with large blue eyes. I hadn't seen Santa Claus since I was a child and was delighted. Santa Claus bowed before me and gave me two presents, one for "baby Seel" with a cute white fluffy bonnet, and one for "Mrs. Seel" with three Swiss handkerchiefs. This was very nice of him and I thanked him and shook his hand...
>
> Georg wrote a long and happy letter. When Bob Nelson and Mrs. Nelson had brought him the telegram many people had been there and they emptied a big bottle to the health of my baby.

It would take Else several weeks to return to Wistaria because of winter conditions and other circumstances. At Hazelton on January 2, she wrote: "I will go home in a week, first to Mrs. Henkel's where Georg will pick me up.

A view of the reserve at Old Hazelton. Else Seel photograph. University of Victoria Archives 4-6-35

Now he is on his way to Seel Lake to get a few marten because we don't have a penny!"

At François Lake, on January 22, Else wrote about her journey from Hazelton.

> On January 10 I had left the hospital. Georg Hauck, a German, took me to the train station. I was almost shaking with nervousness; I was worried about the baby that was brought all of a sudden from the overheated room into the cold winter night, but he slept peacefully through the entire train ride.
>
> At 2 a.m. I got off the train with my child in Burns Lake. Ruddy, the hotel keeper, greeted me in a military fashion, as if he wanted to pay tribute to me for coming back with a son in my arms! The room was icy cold and the windows completely frozen! All night long I held the baby in my arms and couldn't sleep, even though I was exhausted and still weak. Early in the morning I ran to the kitchen where the Chinese cook gave me some warm water. When I washed little Rupert he cried and turned blue. For a moment I was shocked and wanted to lie down next to him and cry, because I thought he was going to

Dr. Horace Wrinch and the hospital at Hazelton are well known in the history of northwestern BC. Else Seel photograph. University of Victoria Archives 4-4-15

> die or get sick. But then I got my strength back, dressed him in warm, clean clothes, and carried him to the maids' room, the only warm room in the hotel. The girls were all very nice and good to us. Rupert was warm and protected in their bed and slept, and I could relax.

Around noon, "I ran a few errands, and then the young McKenna came and took me by car to Mrs. Henkel. Once I got there I took my boy into my arms and put him to my breast. I felt calm again and looked at the green plants and the sun coming in and thought that I would finally be able to sleep, since I had not slept for a full hour at a time since the baby was born."

At the Henkel residence on François Lake, George came to visit her.

> Georg came for one day, through the deep snow, with dog and suitcase. He went right to the boy and wanted to kiss him, with ice on his beard, and I had to hold him back. During the night he came down, gave him the bottle and was delighted how the child could suck. I think he will be a good father and I am happy about that. The next day he took the ferry across François Lake to have a beer at Johnny Keefe's and didn't come back! He met Charley

> Moore who was on his way to Wistaria by sled and he joined him to get back to hunting more quickly, since the hunting season this year will only last until end of February. So dog and suitcase stayed with me and I was alone again for some time. Since Mrs. H. wanted to go to Prince Rupert I had to leave.
>
> Fortunately temperatures rose from –40°C to –10°C. François Lake had just frozen over. Mr. Pringle [the provincial Game Warden] came over in his old Ford, which he had fitted with a long pole between the wheels, in case he would break through the ice. "If you take the chance," because he wanted to take me and the baby across. Why not? So we sped across the ice, over some open cracks that even the dogs would barely dare to cross. I closed my eyes and already saw myself with the child, Mr. Pringle and the car crash through the ice and disappear in the depths of the lake like in a gaping mouth—but we arrived safely in Southbank and Alice Keefe carried the child into the house.
>
> In the evening Keefe's four little girls stood around excitedly around the little boy, whispered delightedly in English and played "baby" until they had to go to bed.

The next morning, Else embarked on the next stage of her return journey, this time by sleigh with Norman Schreiber.

> Like North Pole explorers we left the next morning around 9 a.m. for Ootsa Lake. It was freezing cold; our breath froze on our coats; I was wearing Jonny Keefe's lamb skin. However, the sun shone warmer and warmer, and the horses were steaming and trotting through the magnificent, pristine forest. Many moose tracks crossed the road, the mighty firs had thick snow caps, the bushes were covered in frost and the snow sparkled in the sunlight. What a wonderful winter landscape.
>
> We stopped in Grassy Plains and had lunch at Boström's. Mr. B. is from Sweden who made money with the railway construction and now had the biggest farm in the area... Then we went on. Mr. Schreiber was very concerned about the baby and drove the horses on, so that we would get to his house before sunset. We arrived around 5 p.m.; I was frozen so stiff that I couldn't get off the sled by myself. Now I have been in this house already for one week, our first stop after arriving on Ootsa Lake.

On February 13, from the Schreiber's home at Ootsa Lake, Else wrote. "Still not at home! The bold amazon gave us her own bedroom and Rupert drinks and sleeps, drinks and sleeps, and gains one pound every week."

Dicky Schreiber. Else Seel photograph. University of Victoria Archives 4-4-17

A week later she wrote in her diary: "Still not home! Every day I think that Georg is coming but he stays away. During the last 4 months I have only seen him for 4 days! It is strange: like a stranger he appears sometimes, brings a few stormy days and nights and is gone again. And am I not deep inside happy about it? I am not made for anything permanent, my nature is more of a variable kind."

By late February, Else was back in Wistaria. On March 6, she wrote:

> At home! The horses had trotted faithfully through wind and snow, making their way to our little house. I put the child in Georg's arms and he carried him into the house. Mrs. Schreiber got the best of the three martens that Georg had caught and I was allowed to order a rocking chair, which was more for the baby than for me. It is my first rocking chair, but here in America one cannot be without it. It is rocking back and forth everywhere I go, and I am sure it is not as "lonely" as the one in Christian Morgenstern's poem. [Morgenstern was a German poet who wrote a short poem titled "The Rocking Chair on the Deserted Terrace." It was included in a collection called *Gallows Songs*.]

March 10 was Sunday, so Else went to the post office:

> When I came back two sleds stopped in front of my door and Siwashes stood there. At first I got scared but I don't run away anymore. They wanted to talk to me and see "pictures." I showed them Mrs. Tyee and especially Skin Tyee himself, since

> they were his two sons Johnny and Robert Skin with their wives and children. Johnny Skin spoke English and showed the photograph of his old father to his children who were standing in front of the door with dog pups in their arms. In the guttural voice of his language he probably said to them something like "grandfather." The children looked only briefly and without any comment at this "grandfather" who had been dressed in such good clothes by the institution in Victoria that they would barely bring back a memory of the old wild chief Skin Tyee who wandered through the woods with his gun and wanted to shoot all white people who took away his hunting grounds, declared him crazy and put him in that institution. "You write" Johnny said trustingly "if father is dead." So I had to sit down and write an inquiry to Victoria if the old Skin Tyee was still alive or dead. The "squaw" had brought a basket full of braided things, moccasins etc. with her. I chose two little baskets made from tree bark and asked "how much?" but all she wanted was "old clothes." So I gave her a brown dress, a hat and an apron that Aunt Emma or someone else had embroidered. All this is now going with those "savages."

(Else is probably referring again to the incident with the priest who had referred to "savages" the previous year. Clothes that Else had brought from Germany were being given to First Nations people, but Else freely exchanged them for items made by the Skin family.)

Skin Tyee had been involved in several confrontations with settlers and First Nations people. After an altercation with a settler in which he was severely beaten, Skin Tyee was sent to Essondale (later called Riverview), the provincial government's mental health institution in Coquitlam. Tyee died there in the summer of 1929.

Else also commented: "Georg is not back yet even though he wanted to go away for only 10 days. I wrote an article about Hazelton but it all seems so unemotional after I edited out the only personal part about giving birth."

George returned in mid-March, ending his trapping season a little earlier than usual so that he could prepare for a full season of work on the mine. Else wrote on April 8:

> Georg is here, the first time for a longer period of time. He built a boat for the company and then chopped wood since he never has time for this during the summer...

Mrs. Skin Tyee and a granddaughter. Else Seel photograph. University of Victoria Archives 4-4-03

> Easter [March 31] passed quickly. This time I painted Easter eggs for Georg, one with "Papa Georg"; on mine I just wrote "Else," not "Mama." Harrison's children also got their eggs again, and also Gwenny [Cummins], who visits me so often.
>
> One evening I went to the small schoolhouse. Miss Stone had invited me to attend a small event. There were a dozen school children and they sang "Oh Canada," then they sang songs and performed a short play.

Else started her diary entry for April 26 with a description of a visit by some First Nations people.

> Three Indians just came by to bring me a wild duck. I served them tea and cookies and they drank the tea by bringing the teacup with the saucer up to their mouths. All three were sightly men, well dressed and spoke good English... Bit by bit I get to like the local tribes.

She also wrote about George's departure to the mine.

> One week ago today Georg went with five men to the Tahtsa River. On our porch hung big hams and slabs of bacon, pails of lard and crates of eggs and milk churns were stacked up. It's incredible how much the men eat here. First Jack Leni, the quiet and thoughtful former Iceland fisherman arrived, then McCuish, a prospector and trapper who had been here for 6 years and then had to disappear. He was tall and quiet, with grey hair, and listened to everything that had happened in the meantime. Later, after he had discovered the corner with my books he asked me about Haeckel, Shaw, Darwin and Dostoyevsky. He reads and reads and is also writing somewhere. He doesn't like to move much and sits in the same spot all evening. Than Van Tyne came...
>
> Van Tyne was overly polite, starting each sentence with "yes, Ma'm" and playing the gentleman by cooking and sweeping up. In the evening Dunc McGibbon arrived, thin and quick, drawing his bad foot behind him. It was a long evening with talking about prospecting and mining. Georg said that this area would now rise like the sun and I hope it will, as I cannot indefinitely just sit here and wait.
>
> When I got up the next morning all the dishes were washed and the floors swept. I smiled, thinking about the men in the old country who would never touch anything to do with household tasks.

At the end of May, Else wrote about George's return. "Georg came back a week ago. It was windy and already dark so that I didn't hear the engine but only the scraping of the boat on the gravel when he came ashore. He was beaming and very excited when he showed me his catch: 3 huge beaver furs and a fox that he had found dead—probably poisoned—in front of a cabin. The five other men had lit a fire at the other shore and slept outside."

They worked outside in the garden for a week while Copp was waiting at Ootsa Lake to return to the mine with two boats. They were planning to leave again on Sunday morning. Else wrote:

> Sunday morning Georg left in the empty boat and came back with a heavy load. Mr. Copp greeted me and brought a present for Rupert, a nice blanket with teddy bears; it lays on the blanket for the miners and the cute little stove. Half an hour later

> everything was out on the lake again, and I could only see them with the binoculars. I was left alone as always.

Else described a picnic at Streatham in early June:

> Ed. H[arrison] took us in his boat; I carried Rupert in a basket. As soon as we arrived, Henry T, the "Frenchman," as they call him, took the basket with the baby on his shoulders and went to the picnic place where he was greeted enthusiastically, since everyone had thought the basket contained sandwiches.
>
> There was running and jumping, sack races and ice cream, and despite a few rain showers everyone was in high spirits. Rupert watched the people with big eyes and later slept in the tent, surrounded by a group of young and very young children that all seemed to be fascinated with the baby.

In July, Gwenny Cummins, who was twelve years old, died from a ruptured appendix. Else wrote: "How often she came bringing me mail and fresh milk, swung on to her little horse, and galloped away, her long red hair flying in the wind." Else went to visit the family. She described how the earth was fresh from the rain, the wild red strawberries grew, and from the trees drops of rain fell with the last rays of sun glistening on them. While returning home, she turned several times to see if Gwenny was following her. Almost everyone from Wistaria and the area attended the funeral.

On the last day of August Else wrote: "Georg has not been here for 6 weeks but he wrote a few letters. They work on the tunnel day and night and hope to hit the vein any time. But the rock is very hard and they make only little progress."

Douglas Lay visited the Tahtsa Mining Company's site again during the summer and reported on developments for the Department of Mines.

> **1929**
>
> Good progress has been made during the year at this property by the Tahtsa Mining Company, Limited, with a small force of men (about nine) under the direction of C. L. Copp, Managing Director. A river camp has been constructed on a backwater of the Tahtsa River a few miles below the Emerald Landing, also a mine camp at elevation of 4,245 feet [1295 metres], in timber. The two camps are connected by a good pack trail about 3 ½ miles [5.6 kilometres] in length.

Working crew for the mine. University of Victoria Archives 4-6-33

A view of the Emerald Glacier mine with Rhine Crag in the background on the left. Bureau of Mines photograph. Royal BC Museum, BC Archives J-00864

At elevation 4895 feet [1490 metres] a tunnel had been run a distance of 154 feet [47 metres] to September 27th to develop at a vertical depth of 100 feet [30 metres] the original discovery of mineral on the surface. For the first 84 feet [26 metres] the tunnel crosscuts the formation, encounters the vein at this point, and follows it for the remaining distance. It is stated that a seam of mineral about 3 inches [7.5 centimetres] in width was continuous on the hanging wall for a distance of about 60 feet [18 metres]. A sample of this mineral taken from the floor of the tunnel assayed: gold, trace; silver, 23 oz. [652 grams] to the ton; lead, nil; zinc, trace. The assay disclosed the presence of a large amount of arsenic. The mineral is grey-black in colour and may be arsenopyrite. The face shows a shear-zone 6 ½ feet [2 metres] in width, slightly mineralized throughout with small amounts of galena and zinc-blende. In another 40 feet [12 metres] this tunnel will be immediately below the surface showing. This shear-zone outcrops on the surface at a point 165 feet [50 metres] vertically below the tunnel and is well mineralized at this point, where a width of 10 inches [25 centimetres] of mixed galena and zinc-blende shows. A sample of this assayed: gold, 0.01 oz. [0.283 grams] to the ton; silver,

> 95 oz [2693 grams] to the ton; lead 19.5 per cent; zinc, 10.6 per cent; copper, trace. It is stated that another parallel shear-zone was discovered during the year at a point about 750 feet [230 metres] east of that under development, which is very similar to the latter.

While he was in the area, Lay also visited the nearby Emerald Glacier mine. It was a busy summer for mining activity, as the Burns Lake *Observer* reported on August 15.

> **Big staking boom hits district**
>
> **Every area is being covered by prospectors and many companies have paid men in field**
>
> Nearly all the rural population has turned to prospecting and left their plowshares and hay and crops while they join the rush to stake hard minerals. Nor is the rush confined to any one point, for all the area from Big Eutsuk and Whitesail Lake to François Lake, Nadina and Owen Lake is being actively combed over and staked in many promising locations. Excellent showings are being made at many points...
>
> Including the regular prospectors and local farmers and business men who have got the fever, there are to be found also a number of men paid by several large companies, who are on the ground floor to pick up what they can in stakings for their various companies.
>
> It is remarkable that this district should show such ores, much of which is on the beaten track of traffic and has been available for years. Nearly every mineral is represented in the various claims and some of the ores are of a nature to stump the field man when it comes to stating what they are. Much sampling has been done and assays are awaited with expectancy. The results of some of these, when known, will no doubt create considerable excitement.
>
> The big companies have their interest directed toward this district now, and a better time to stake and prospect could not be asked for.

Since the Tahtsa Mining Company's property was in a remote area and it was difficult to access the main transportation routes from there, George experimented with an unusual method of shipping his ore samples, as the

Burns Lake *Observer* reported on September 5.

> **Airplane will freight out rich ore from Whitesail property**
>
> Making the trip from Stewart, a distance of 375 miles [600 kilometres] in two hours and twenty minutes, the hydroplane "Pintail" landed in Burns Lake last Sunday en route to Whitesail Lake where it is proposed to chart the course preparatory to shipping out by plane the exceedingly rich ore on the Seel property. This is a project which has been under consideration for some time and experts are of the opinion that by bringing out the ore by plane to Burns Lake for rail shipment there will still be left a large margin of profit after all transportation charges are paid.
>
> This will constitute an innovation in the shipment of ores and the experiment will be watched with considerable interest. The mine is situated 70 air miles [112 kilometres] from Burns Lake. The plane is owned by the Western Canada Airways and was in charge of Fergie Macdonald. The mine which was discovered and staked by George Seel of Wistaria has long been known to produce some of the richest ore in the province.

The Prince George *Citizen* also reported on Seel's flight and its potential significance. The newspaper noted: "There is said to be a large quantity of high-grade ore uncovered in the Seel property which was discovered by George Seel of Wistaria, but it promises to be very difficult to serve it by either water or road transportation. If a good sample can be brought out by the plane the capital to provide the necessary transportation will doubtless be found. The mine is distant 70 air miles [112 kilometres] from Burns Lake." The paper also commented: "While the transportation of ore by plane will be an expensive method the use of the planes is expected to speed up the mining operations in the out-of-the-way districts. Burns Lake affords good facilities for hydro and land planes virtually within the town limits and a gas service station is being installed to cater to their requirements."

George's plan for transporting the ore samples never materialized because the stock market crash in October led to the Great Depression.

CF-ABB THE *PINTAIL*

Frank Swannell took this photograph of the *Pintail* (one of the few existing pictures of this plane) in June 1929 at Finlay Forks. Royal BC Museum, BC Archives I-58144

In an article in the Burns Lake *Observer* on February 7, 1929, Western Canada Airways announced the purchase of two Boeing B-1E flying boats, CF-ABA (*Petrel*) and CF-ABB (*Pintail*). Their primary use would be "for fisheries patrol, photographic flights, sketch mapping of timber areas and such work." That summer the BC government started a large project mainly focused on the Peace River region called the PGE (Pacific Great Eastern) Resources Survey. It included the first extensive aerial photography mapping ever done in the province. Most of the photography was taken by Royal Canadian Air Force airplanes, but the two flying boats also worked on the project. Frank Swannell, one of the government surveyors, took some photographs of the *Pintail* at Finlay Forks early in the summer.

After completing its work in the Peace River region, the two airplanes were moved to Stewart in the late summer. Shortly after transporting a shipment of Seel's ore, the *Pintail* participated in a dramatic incident that started at the Emerald Glacier mine across the valley. The incident was reported in the Burns Lake newspaper on September 12 and carried by several newspapers in Canada.

Consolidated Mining & Smelting Company sends plane to take wounded man to Vancouver

H. C. Hughes, mining engineer of the Consolidated Mining & Smelting Co., following an old lead in Sibola mountain vicinity, near Ootsa Lake last week, surprised a large grizzly bear, which was but nine feet [3 metres] distant. The bear immediately attacked, striking Hughes on the hip and knocking him several feet. With presence of mind Hughes feigned death, keeping his face down and covered by his arm as much as possible. The bear tore his face and leg and bit him in the shoulder and back of the neck and broke the bone in one finger. After a few minutes the bear left his victim and Hughes walked ten miles [16 kilometres] to camp. He was rushed by boat and car to Burns Lake Hospital and arrived on Thursday night. The hospital was full up, but Rev. W. R. Ashford took the injured man into the United Church Manse.

Infection set in in the wounds and on Tuesday night the company employing Mr. Hughes sent a seaplane here from Stewart [the *Pintail*] which landed in Burns Lake at 7 p.m. On Wednesday morning the plane left with the injured man, accompanied by Miss Scott, R. N. of the Burns Lake hospital staff... Pilot Wm. Gilbert was in charge of the plane and Geo. Taylor is the mechanic.

The *Petrel* flew until 1933 and the *Pintail* operated until 1935.

On September 18, Else wrote: "After 6 weeks, Georg came back on Sunday, September 1. He sold 30,000 shares, but for only $3,000, but at least we have something. The other half is only to speculate. As a gift he gave me 10,000 shares and $1,000 to go to Berlin." She commented that "Georg stayed home for an entire week that went by really quickly."

After George left, two German men came for a visit. Else took Rupert and went with them on a two-day trip to Marilla at the eastern end of Ootsa Lake. This was her first visit to that part of the lake.

> After lunch I went with Kurt [Unger] and Albert and Rupert at high speed to Ootsa Lake and from there along the shore, and up a real path, with a wonderful view of both ends of the Ootsa Lake.

> Through a dark forest with thick, high trunks we went to the fairy tale castle, that is in reality Jimmy Harrison's log cabin [not related to the Harrisons at Wistaria]. Two nice days in the wild west and a bit of "Berlin flirting" with Kurt U. who had moved from Berlin, from the western part of town, to this wild west when he was 17 years old. [Kurt Unger was the son of a German woman who lived near François Lake.]

They stayed overnight at the Ootsa Lake settlement and then took a day trip to the eastern end of the lake.

> A whole day on the water. We made tea on the beach and picked red berries while the men hunted grouse. Then, at the end of the Ootsa Lake [Marilla] a big store only for the Indians and the Henson family. Him and her and three sons... They had a big elegant house with wallpaper, linoleum, wooden floors and nice paintings on the walls that Grell had painted, the former

Jimmy Andrews and family. Else Seel photograph. University of Victoria Archives 4-4-25

> bandit who once had saved Georg from the police... A painting of Indians throwing rocks at a bear looked so much like the type of painting that I had seen in the Bavarian mountains. There was also a self-portrait of Grell that he had begun shortly before his death but not finished. A friend had later added the teeth that were supposed to make this wild man with his long hair and beard look more friendly, but I thought it made him look like a grinning skull. Poor Grell, he drowned in the Tahtsa River when his boat tipped over. Georg, who happened to pass by could only rescue Grell's friend Mr. Dawson, who has now also died.

When Else returned, she had visitors.

> After I was home again and had everything organized a big car came and McAdam and McDonnell got out. They wanted to go to the mine and wait here for van Tyne who wanted to pick them up by boat. They had all come by plane from Stewart, where they have another mine working. McDonnell, fat, sweating and friendly and McAdam, gaunt and quiet with a briefcase: business men. They fetched wood and water and McAdam dug up some potatoes that I cooked for them for dinner. In between, a small lecture about the annuity bank, Zeppelins and the "Bremen," the "Blue Ribbon of the Ocean." When they left two days later at midnight they wrote down their Vancouver address and asked me to visit them so that I could show them Vancouver and I said that I would rather show them Berlin. By the way, they took ore with them by the sackfuls right away. "Plain silver" said Georg who returned a week later. [McAdam and McDonnell were mine promoters.]

In her diary entry for October 12, she described a visit from Jimmy Andrews and his wife:

> who brought me baskets made from birch bark, and moccasins for Rupert. I gave her a dress that she pulled [on] right away over all her other clothes. The dress was copper and jade coloured, with an Egyptian hieroglyphs pattern and suited the Indian woman with her red skin and black hair wonderfully, like it was made for her. Then I told them that I would go far, far away in the winter, half way around the world. To explain

> it to them I showed them a small globe that I had bought for 10 cents from a street merchant in Berlin and showed them the route I would travel: through all of Canada and over the Atlantic to Europe.

She also wrote about George's return almost a week earlier.

> Georg and Mr. Copp came at midnight on Sunday. They were frozen stiff, being on the water all day and the nights are now already very cold. I heard the engine, jumped out of bed, put the lamp into the window and started cooking what I had. They warmed themselves up, ate, and talked about this land where the wheat freezes and the soil consists mainly of glacial wash. I wanted to bring people here, but they said that only Peace River is good for farming. Then bring in at least artists—painters—the landscape is beautiful.
>
> The next day Mr. Copp wanted to go to Vancouver and took my beaver fur. Georg came from Ootsa Lake in the afternoon and in the evening we went across country to Jack Shelford, who, as notary public, completed the forms for the passport.

In early January of 1930, Else and Rupert departed for Germany. As they left, the effects of the Great Depression were starting to become noticeable. The decade of prosperity following World War I was coming to a close.

Subsistence

The Great Depression, which started in the fall of 1929 and lasted through the 1930s, affected the economy of many countries of the world, particularly those in Europe and North America. Dust bowl conditions impacted agriculture on the Canadian Prairies and the American Great Plains. There was a high rate of unemployment. People who lived in urban centres and depended on employment income were particularly impacted by the loss of jobs or reduced wages. As Christopher Beach describes in his thesis, the settlement at Ootsa was also affected, but not nearly to the same extent. Settlers still had their farms for raising crops, and the surrounding environment provided game, fish and berries. The settlers were used to helping each other and were not as dependent on cash to sustain themselves. The government provided roadwork for the men so that they could pay the taxes on their land and maintain their farms. Trapping still continued, but reduced prices for furs meant less income. Individual co-operative arrangements with the Cheslatta Carrier Nation were maintained.

The Depression also had a psychological impact on many people. Financial worries and the inability to see better prospects for the future created personal depression. Else's diaries reflected these concerns. She wrote less frequently during the 1930s, and when she wrote, she was worried about the family's economic condition and the welfare of the children. At times she thought about moving elsewhere, but she realized that would probably not improve the family's situation. As it was for most other people who lived through the Depression, the 1930s was a decade of subsistence and persistence for the Seel family. During this time, support from neighbours and a connection to the locale where they lived played an important role for George, Else and their children.

Else used some of the money from George's sale of shares in the mine to take a six-month trip to Europe with Rupert. Most of the time was spent

Else and Rupert in Germany. University of Victoria Archives 4-5-03

visiting her family in Berlin. Else took a trip to Pomerania where she grew up, and also travelled to France for a week.

At the end of March, she visited the Rentenbank, her former place of employment. Else was glad to see people she knew, but realized that little had changed since she had left over two years earlier. She commented on the oppressive atmosphere.

> The pictures hung in the same spots, the furniture was still in the same place. Miss Heines sat now at my desk. There were more books now, the shelves were filled and I was touched by seeing my own hand writing here and there. But the air in the room was stuffy and hard to breathe. It seemed impossible to me to come back here and sit down and do this work like flies under a glass cover. No, it wouldn't be possible—my beloved Ootsa Lake.

While Else was in Europe, George maintained his way of life at Ootsa. During the winter he trapped, but the drop in fur prices brought less income. He planted a garden but it was not as productive. Since the price of silver, one of the main minerals in George's mining claims, had decreased, there was no investment money to continue work. The only mine in the area that remained in operation was the Emerald Glacier. It was further developed and the Consolidated Mining and Smelting Company had sufficient financial resources to continue work in hopes that the Depression would not last too long.

Else's first diary entry after she returned was on September 3. She wrote that George was very happy to see her, and he had painted the two rooms of the house while she was away. Else was worried that life would become more difficult.

Else and Rupert on the ship. University of Victoria Archives 4-5-17

> Times are hard over there. Everything stagnates and is turbulent, and the seven lean years have started: here in B.C. they brought heat and drought, a bad harvest and huge forest fires. Mrs. Schreiber caught up with me, still being the same Amazon that she was three years ago. But on the right and on the left the grass was withered, and ahead, at the horizon, the fiery clouds were rising. My big red cape was wafting around my shoulders and I sang wildly and sadly whatever came to my mind—what times were those that I was facing—they were not quiet ones. Georg, however, sat blissfully holding the boy in his arms.
>
> Rupert is asleep, the bread is baking in the oven, Georg is in the mountains looking for gold and I write, which most certainly is pointless, but the only thing that I can do. Outside is Ootsa Lake with the mountains behind it. They are beckoning, and I finally want to go there; even if I have to carry the child on my back, as the Indian women do it.

A few weeks later George had a serious accident at the site of his mining claims. The Burns Lake *Observer* described the incident in a September 25 article.

Wistaria prospector hurled twenty feet in explosion

George Seel is terribly burned when gasoline lamp explodes and ignites his clothing and cabin. Suffering horrible burns he battles all night to reach home at Wistaria

George Seel, Wistaria prospector and rancher, had a marvelous escape from death last Tuesday night and it is only due to quick presence of mind and abundant energy and nerve that he lives to tell the tale today. He was up at his cabin in the Whitesail and had just lit the gasoline lamp and proceeded to hang the lamp from a hook in the ceiling. Thinking that the lamp was on the hook, he released it and the lamp fell to the floor. The stem of the lamp broke off and the pressure caused the gas to spurt in a fountain over the room and the occupant. It instantly ignited and Seel was a mass of flames. He seized some canvas and wrapped it around himself, making his way through the blazing room, without breathing, to the door. In order to unlatch the door he had to uncover one arm and as he did this the gas in that portion of the covering exploded, by some peculiar circumstance stripping all the skin off the arm from the elbow to the wrist. There were 15,000 dynamite caps and blasting powder in the cabin and before Seel had proceeded but a short distance these exploded, throwing him down the hill for about twenty feet.

There was no one in the district to Mr. Seel's knowledge and suffering terrible agony, with his face and head badly burned, all the skin off his arm in addition to many other dreadful burns, Mr. Seel had the temerity and fortitude to make his way down to his boat and all night fought the pain while he made his way to his home nine miles down Ootsa Lake. He reached there in a semi-delirious and exhausted condition on Wednesday morning.

His wife, who returned home from a visit to Germany only a few weeks ago, rendered first aid and called Dr. Holmes who arrived on the scene on Thursday morning and the victim is now gradually recovering from the shock and in a short time will take a skin-grafting treatment in hospital.

Else wrote about George's accident in her diary on October 6.

> He came back three weeks ago. As always I happily ran outside when I heard the boat and saw that his face was wrapped in flour sacks and his arm was bandaged. His eyes were swollen and his whole face burnt. Back in the house I washed him and took off the bandages. Blood, dead skin and blood clots; it was terrible. The arm was even worse: raw flesh and deep holes. Georg had been in the mining cabin to get tools and provisions. He wanted to stay overnight and hung the gasoline lamp on its usual hook. The hook fell off, the lamp exploded and within seconds everything was in flames. The cabin was full of dynamite and Georg lashed about with a tarpaulin and tried to open the door with closed eyes, burning his left hand so badly in the process. When he was just 20 feet away from the cabin it exploded. Rocks and trees were flying around. Only the heavy rain prevented a huge forest fire. The huge air pressure from the explosion put out the flames on Georg. It was midnight and under horrible pain he went from the mountain to the river cabin and left early in the morning to come back here where he arrived at 4 p.m. When he was lying in bed he started to get cold and weak. I went over to the Harrison's to ask them to phone the doctor in Burns Lake from the post office phone but they couldn't reach him and he didn't come until the next afternoon.

Else didn't know or trust the doctor.

> However, he couldn't make things worse; scraped the dead skin off the face and arm, all with the same water and he hadn't even washed his hands. With yellow salve he stuck bandages to Georg's face. The first week was bad: Georg was in a lot of pain and I had to toil away doing housework, because visitors kept on coming and even stayed overnight and I had to bake cakes and bread and set and clean the table just like it was a festive event. Now the bandages are off the face and still on the arm, but he is able to saw wood again.

George eventually recovered and was able to resume working. Else described the changing economic conditions, but emphasized the positive aspects of their situation.

> We only got two sacks of potatoes and one sack of carrots from our garden. We usually get three or four times as much. But there are bad times here too. Wheat prices are down, furs even more so and silver is even more worthless. It's all over. Last year at this time there was so much optimism and 3000 dollars on top of that. Only half of that is left now and it will get less and less until we have to live from hand to mouth again. But we don't care much about that. The most important thing is that we are healthy and busy, busy with things to do and things that keep our minds busy.

George started trapping in early November. In a detailed diary entry on November 23, Else wrote that three weeks of trapping produced only one mink worth about ten dollars. George and Else decided that it might be easier and more productive to start a beaver farm. The Eddings had a mink farm, and the Shelfords raised foxes, so they thought that raising beaver might prove profitable for them. Else recorded that "Georg got tree trunks and posts and cut wood to build tanks and a wind turbine. It will take 6 months to build and then another 2 months in June and July to get the beavers."

Baptiste assisted George and Else.

> The Indian Baptiste brought a beaver net and offered his help to catch the animals alive... They [Baptiste's family] camped here in our bay and when I brought them shoes and such things they were sitting by the fire in front of their tent. The children lay on fir branches that were covered with bear skins and moose meat was hanging in the trees. Now they go for the winter to their cabin on Tahtsa Lake and live on the fish they catch. In the spring they come back with their canoe and go to the mountains.

Else also described the situation regarding the Emerald Mine.

> Last Sunday in the dark and during a snowstorm all of a sudden the "Emerald" landed, the big boat of the Consolidated Mining and Smelting Co. Van Tyne had seen our light and came lured to it like a moth. With him was Hughes, the chief engineer. That meant cooking a big supper and after there were talks about mines, the country and its people. Hughes was very pessimistic and said that there is no ore here and that there are only two good mines in B.C.,

the "Premier" and the "Big Missouri" [both large gold mines near Stewart in northwestern BC]. He thought our mine was better than the "Emerald" but what does that mean? We didn't hear anything from Copp. Hughes is tired of having to live up there for a 4th year and since ore was only found at the entrance the mine will probably be closed soon. A big loss for this area which will become as dead again as it was before.

But the beavers will live and become tame and multiply—hopefully. Then on my next visit to Berlin I can offer my "real Canadian beavers" to Dr. Heck at the zoo and become famous by raising beavers instead of by writing novels.

On Christmas day, Else wrote about the holiday season at Wistaria.

We had a goose and a sort of punch that I had managed to brew. Pearl [Henson] had brought the goose yesterday...

The Christmas tree in Wistaria seemed inappropriate this year. There was no singing and the kids were not reciting anything. They were supposed to have costumes, but nobody was dressed up, except for Alice Nelson as a flower girl who was wearing the artificial flowers that I had brought from Germany for funeral wreaths and that were now used for a better purpose, and two of the Shelford boys who were playing Wilhelm Tell and son. One of them was wearing a cap with a quilted apple sewn onto it...

As always there was a dance and Rupert stomped his feet and wanted to follow me, so that Georg had to hold him back.

In Streatham, on the other hand, there was a lot of singing again, almost too long for the children. It was heart-warming to see how those 3 to 4 families made an effort to provide some "artistic" education for the 10 children. They are all English families from the old country and tried to bring some of the "old culture" over here.

She described the work that they did for the fur farm.

The beaver farm makes progress. A big area is fenced in, with the fence going half a meter deep into the ground. A big tank lined with planks, making a nice swimming pool right next to the house with two bedrooms and dining room with a flap to put in the food, mostly willow and turnips, but also apples and

> rice pudding which the beavers also like, as Grey Owl says... I wonder if our beavers can also be tamed. I will do my best and I look forward to getting the animals.

Else described the scene at their home.

> Rupert blows out the candles on the Christmas tree and cracks nuts. The squirrel gets some too, it picks them up from the window sill. There is not a lot of snow and not a trace of ice on the lake. Ravens just flew by, big and fat like geese. Little chickadees flit around and peck at our big quarters of beef.

She also wrote about guests who were coming to visit them.

> Tomorrow Mohrs will be coming to visit. He is the son of a shoemaker from the Rhineland and she is the daughter of a tailor from Königsberg. They were both born in the USA but speak German well, so I will speak German to them. We will eat well, let the gramophone play and talk of this and that. New society with old customs. Later in the evening Georg, the farmer's son from Bavaria, will play the zither and finally, when everybody's gone home, I, the estate's owner's daughter from Pomerania, will wash the dishes and sweep the floor.

Amidst all the gloomy economic news in 1930, there was an article in the *Winnipeg Tribune* on July 29 that was a precursor to a major event that would transform the lives of most of the settlers and Cheslatta residents two decades later.

> *Victoria—July 29*
>
> **Notable Water Power Sites Found in BC**
>
> **Engineers Foresee Possible 1,200,000 Horsepower in Coast District**
>
> The greatest water powers in Canada, greater even than those harnessed along the St. Lawrence, have been revealed along the coast of British Columbia, north of Vancouver, by government engineers during the past summer, it is stated at parliament buildings here.
>
> Preliminary reports received here indicate in addition to the noted Taseko-Chilco-Homathko Power, with a possible

> development of 1,200,000 horsepower, two other sources of electricity have been discovered, bringing the possible development of the Coast district up to the large figure of three million horsepower.
>
> The two new power sites revealed by recent surveys are at Tahtsa and Eutsuk Lake. By turning the water of these lakes westward, instead of eastward into the Fraser, engineers believe that 1,800,000 horsepower can be harnessed.

In the 1920s, the British Columbia government began exploring the possibility of hydroelectric power projects along the Coast Mountains. In some locations the mountains were not far from the ocean, so there was a considerable elevation change from the Interior in a relatively short distance. The initial focus was the large lakes of the southern Chilcotin plateau (Chilco, Taseko and Tatlayoko) and the Homathko River, which flowed into Bute Inlet on the Central Coast.

Frank Swannell completed his government surveying project on the east side of the Coast Mountains in 1928. The maps he produced showed that the lakes on the headwaters of the Nechako were over 800 metres in elevation and not far from the ocean. In addition, there was a canyon on the Nechako River below the lakes of the Great Circle route where a dam could be built to block the flow of the water. From the western end of Eutsuk Lake there were a couple of passes through the mountains. Tahtsa Lake, which was less than fifteen kilometres from the ocean, appeared to be a particularly promising location for hydroelectric development. The hydroelectric potential of the upper Nechako was the largest in the province at that time, but it also entailed the most significant alteration of a river drainage in British Columbia.

The BC government's Water Rights Branch began its survey of Tahtsa Lake in 1930 and installed gauges along the Tahtsa River to measure water flow. The Depression precluded any major development of a hydroelectric project, but the Water Rights Branch continued working and monitoring their water flow gauges in the Tahtsa drainage and around Eutsuk Lake throughout the 1930s. During that decade, Bill McNeill received a few government contracts to remove log jams and sweepers from the Tahtsa River, and he usually hired George to help.

Else's first diary entry for 1931 was on January 7.

> The new year came quietly. I stayed up and read *Macleans* magazine and *The National Geographic* magazine, one of the best American magazines, even though no one here has high expectations. Georg and Rupert were already asleep. I was

> thinking of the laughter and merriment in Berlin a year ago and looked out the window at midnight; the Ootsa Lake was still full and fresh without a trace of ice. It was a clear and warm night, and the moon was passing by. So now it's 1931!

She wrote about life around their home.

> A squirrel lives in the extension that will be the kitchen but still looks the same as when I came back. Georg doesn't have any time, he works on the beaver farm all the time. One box is ready and he hopes to bring in a beaver soon. He is in the mountains again and wants to go over his trap line 4 times since for the past 6 months we live only on the mining money in the bank. Add on expenses for boards and wire and we have only $500 left, but there were times when we had nothing.

Ootsa Lake was not yet frozen, so Consolidated Mining used the opportunity to close their operation in the Tahtsa drainage. Else wrote that "Dunc McGibbon and van Tyne came with the 'Emerald' and took Georg with them at four o'clock in the morning. It was light as day and the snow shone ghostly as the boat left. The glamour of the mine is done, this boat is going to pick up the last people from the Emerald Mine that the Consolidated Comp[any] has now given up, after they had spent 200,000 dollars. Only gold is of interest now and it is somewhere—but where?"

In the late 1920s, many new roads were built in the Central Interior region. During the Depression, the government provided relief by hiring men for short-term work on roads around the area where they lived. The road was extended from Wistaria towards the Seel property where it turned west towards the residence of Old Bill Harrison. A branch was built to the Shelford ranch, farther west and on the hillside above the lake. Construction of the main road continued northwest, passing along the western shore of François Lake and eventually reaching the community of Houston along the railway line west of Burns Lake. All the roads in the area south of Burns Lake were gravel.

In late January, Else wrote:

> There is a real settlement now around the lake and the road that I so much disagreed with goes now right around our house. In the fall American tourists knocked on our door, asking for tools to repair their car. They made a lot of noise when they drove around the corner on the gravel. Half a dozen lights are

glowing on the shore but not very long, since the people here go to bed at 9 p.m. but it still bothers me. My solitude is gone and I cannot be loud and silly any more like I used to in my first year here.

In her diary for early March, Else noted that the winter was mild, and she commented on the progress made towards the beaver farm during the two weeks that George was home.

Georg brought water in barrels and 80 barrels just filled a few feet in the big tank. He hopes to bring back a beaver this time. He built a sled especially for this purpose.

Rupert also got a sled and we dashed around with him on the Lake. I pull the sleigh as if I were a little horse and pull him to the post office. However, I am not as excited as I used to be to get letters and news; it starts to crumble... I have to grow some roots here, for which I need a good deal of patience which unfortunately I don't have.

Around the house in winter. Else Seel photograph. University of Victoria Archives 4-5-19

One day, during the last week of March, Else was out walking with Rupert in the vicinity of the house.

Then I heard the music box playing, as if by magic. Since I don't believe in magic I went back to the house and found the entire Ed. H[arrison] family there, including their new, five-week-old baby. We talked about the hard times and were happy to be here on the Ootsa Lake. We played German and American records on the gramophone while the sun warmed us like an overcoat. It was wonderful. Mrs. Ed wore shoes and stockings

> with big holes in them and I gave her some from Germany. Her dress was also very shabby, but I don't have any dresses left since I gave my last two to Mrs. Buster H., who had been really happy about it. No, the people cannot buy anything anymore. I can use my German supplies.

Else also wrote: "Georg has been gone for 6 weeks now. I look for him on the horizon with the binoculars."

Else described the arrival of their first beaver in mid-April.

> Georg pushed him like a lady on the sleigh across the ice. The animal looked scared and tried to hide in a corner. We brought the sleigh to the pen which was filled with melted snow and Georg grabbed the beaver by its tail and neck and threw him into the water. He dived and splashed, came up again and looked around, before he found by instinct the entrance to the little hut and disappeared. The first few days he sat quietly in a corner on the hay and wouldn't touch any food. Finally he

The church at Wistaria, April 1931. Both automobiles and a horse and sleigh are visible in the picture. Else Seel photograph. University of Victoria Archives 4-5-20

gnawed at the willow branches and when I checked on him today all bark was gone from the branches.

Since the animal is a three-year-old female I called her "Eva," hoping that she will become the progenitrix of our beaver colony.

Georg has gone to get "Adam." In the meantime an American outfit came, four men and a boss, who drove in his cab around our house every day, making it unsafe for Rupert to be outside. They are building boats at Harrison's saw mill and want to go to Whitesail Lake as soon as the ice is gone and build a lodge for American tourists in the wilderness, with warm and cold showers and other conveniences, like in Jasper Park. The people living by the lake sense the opportunity for income and are optimistic again.

The lodge at Whitesail Lake was constructed, but it did not operate for very long because of the Depression.

Mrs. Louise Nelson (left), Else and Rupert at the post office. University of Victoria Archives 4-5-21

Near the end of the month Copp wrote to George.

> Things are pretty quiet here in the mining line. I have not heard yet if the Consolidated Co'y is going to do anything on the Emerald this year. I hear that the diamond drilling did not prove up much.
>
> The price of silver, lead, zinc and copper are still going down and there does not seem to be much prospect of its rising in the near future. There is some demand for good gold prospects. But they are hard to find. What luck did you have trapping? I see that the Dominion government has stopped Russian furs from coming into Canada. But I do not think it will make much difference with the price of raw furs here...
>
> Write and let me know the news. Trusting this finds you and Mrs. Seel in the best of health.

In early May, Else wrote: "The lake is finally open and the water is rushing again. This time Georg could paddle by boat through the floating ice sheets. I noticed how happy he was to be on the water again." George returned with a second beaver.

> It's another female, but her fur is darker, which means more valuable. I name her "Elsie." At first, she was a lot wilder than the first one, but now she is equally as calm. They even sleep together, even though they have 4 separate rooms in their little house. With their muzzles close together, it seems as if they are seeking comfort and warmth from each other. Yesterday I removed the gnawed-off branches. They eat quite a lot and when I put new willow branches into their pen, they pull them inside and bite them in half. They stack the gnawed-off pieces carefully outside their little cabin. They thrive, get used to everything quickly, and are stoic like old wise people who accept their life.
>
> I am the same: I accept my life. It is a strange stage between 30 and 40; not young and not old. The children grow up and the animals do their duty. The chickens lay eggs, the cow gives milk, I bake bread and cakes, supply food for all the living things and do my duty. But something keeps on asking persistently: Is that everything? It may be just like that—but I cannot grasp it.

Two weeks later George left for a final trip: "Georg is going to get beavers for the 4th time. Last time he was not lucky, but this time he will go far into the Coast Mountains where he has observed a large beaver colony for years."

In June, Else wrote: "Georg is here and built a water pipe to the beaver pen. The beavers feel comfortable, eat a lot, and get along with each other. The female is big and might have pups—that would be nice." Else also wrote about her own pregnancy: "I walk around and feel tied to the earth and primordial times and cannot do anything except let the summer pass and the winter come, and with it the pains of childbirth."

Else wanted to have her second child born at the hospital at Hazelton, even though their finances were limited. At the beginning of August she went by herself for a short trip. First she travelled by train to Prince Rupert. During the five days she spent there, Else had two dentist appointments. She observed that "there are currently 700 people unemployed in Prince Rupert, that's 10% of the population. The government gives them work sometimes in road construction, for a dollar a day plus food." She visited a couple of women that she had met during her trip to the city in 1928, and "Jimmy Morgan from Ootsa Lake came to the hotel. He had shaved and was well dressed. He worked at the dry docks and is now getting by as unemployed."

Else, George and Rupert. University of Victoria Archives 4-5-23

Ploughing the garden. Else Seel photograph. University of Victoria Archives 4-5-23

She stopped at Hazelton on the way back. "Finally I met the old Dr. Wrinch who gave me a photograph of the new 3-story hospital. I told him that I would come there after New Year and he said that he was looking forward to it. I said that I wasn't looking forward to it so much." Then she took the train to Burns Lake where "The hotel in Burns Lake was fully booked and I was lucky to get the last available room. The next day 30 people from the Board of Trade went to Ootsa Lake and I went with them as far as François Lake where Mrs. Keefe had a birthday party for the little Yvonne. One night with the Andersons in Streatham and then back to our little house where Georg was busy boiling potatoes for lunch and Rupert at first seemed so foreign to me for the first few minutes."

One of the government's relief projects at Ootsa Lake in 1931 was the construction of a fair grounds and racetrack. The Burns Lake *Observer* reported on this project in an article on August 20.

> **Stampede committee preparing grounds at Ootsa Lake**
>
> **Race track is being built and corrals and fences erected for Labor Day sports**
>
> The stampede committee is working faster than either the Provincial or Federal Government, having established a relief

> camp on the open prairie surrounding the old Indian graveyard named after the famous (or infamous) Skin Tyee.
>
> The racetrack is being graded and fenced, corrals and chutes built in preparation for the Labor Day Stampede and anyone seeking work can find it by applying at the grounds, carrying their grub and tools, where they will be assured of being relieved of any superfluous energy.
>
> In the heavy growth of timber on the shore line just west of the grounds are many signs of the existence of a large Indian village, probably centuries old, affording a most interesting study for the archaeologist. At fairly regular intervals, deep saucer-like depressions occur, from thirty to forty feet [9 to 12m] in circumference, undoubtedly the site of the lodges of a generation long passed, as the timber growing in some of these depressions shows an age of over one hundred years.

Else described the Labour Day activities that they attended: "There was also a barbeque and a rodeo in Ootsa. The meat, that had been buried in the ground and roasted on hot stones, was delicious. The bronc riding and horse races went on for hours... An airplane with red wings would take people on 10-minute flights for 5 dollars. In the evening, before the dancing began, we went home by boat. The little child inside my womb is already too big to allow me to dance. Rupert was fast asleep in my lap, dead tired after all the great events of the day."

George had spent the summer prospecting in a new area: "Georg was in Kimsquit near the coast where he was looking for potash and found copper with a 'trace of gold,' but only a trace, so that all my hopes for the future sank. I had thought of a summer in Bella Coola with the two children and a Norwegian nanny."

In October, Else wrote about George's difficulties and the depression she was feeling.

> Georg is suffering from rheumatism and from an old wound that he received a long time ago when a rival shot him in the leg. It's still causing him trouble every 2 to 3 years. How difficult men are when they suffer pain. What would they do if they had to bear children? Perhaps they would be more patient. Mrs. Keefe, who had her 6th child 14 days ago, said that she would like to have 3 more, if her husband would give birth to one of them.

> I didn't get to go to the mountains after all; this would have been my last opportunity. Now it's stormy and rainy, and up there it will be snowing. The vastness and the loneliness of the land suck me in. Everything falls off of me, and everything which once was insight, drive and love, becomes void. I don't write any more, I now give birth to children.

On January 3, 1932 Else wrote in her diary: "The new year began without a human sound or human soul. Only a mouse came at midnight and gnawed at the sheepskin rug by my bed. Georg went trapping one more time before I will go away. I am here by myself and helpless, should anything happen in those two weeks before giving birth. We don't have any money left and even owe the store 50 dollars. During the last two months Georg brought a silver fox and we hoped to get a good price for it." With the drop in fur prices during the Depression, George was having difficulty selling the fur.

CF-AAM was a Fokker Super Universal built in 1929 for the Consolidated Mining and Engineering Company. One of their engineers, Emil Bronlund, used it for mineral exploration in northern BC for several years. Bronlund spent part of the summer of 1931 working around Thutade Lake with Frank Swannell. He was returning south at the end of the field season when he stopped at Ootsa Lake. Today CF-AAM has been restored and is housed in the Royal Aviation Museum of Western Canada in Winnipeg. Else Seel photograph. University of Victoria Archives 4-5-24

Else described Rupert's birthday: "He turned three and we celebrated with eight children who came to play and made a lot of noise." She noted: "We have a new kitchen which is a blessing after living and cooking in one room for four years."

By January 18, Else was at Hazelton: "Georg took me to Ootsa Lake by sleigh. It was just getting cold again; two days ago the thermometer had dropped to 28 below zero [−33°C]. We left Rupert with Mrs. Ed. H. and Clark's tired, stiff horses pulled us slowly along." Then she travelled with Norman Schreiber to Burns Lake where she stayed overnight. While there she sold the silver fox for fifty dollars along with some other furs George had trapped. The next afternoon the train left Burns Lake, arriving at Hazelton after midnight. In her diary she wrote "Now come quickly you little baby—I already dreamed that you were there and someone brought a white hyacinth, as high as the sky, to honour you. But then I woke up and my body was still heavy and full, and my heart listened anxiously into the night."

A daughter, Gloria Regina, was born on January 28. Else remained at Hazelton for two more weeks. She wrote on March 22:

> We left Hazelton on February 10. The road to the station was covered in snow. The car glided through a quiet landscape...

The new hospital in Hazelton constructed in 1931. Else Seel photograph. University of Victoria Archives 4-5-26

> All the log cabins were peacefully nestled together. Once before had I taken this road back to life, with a baby in my arms. Back then with Rupert, now with Gloria.
>
> Two children! They both lie in their cribs now and breathe peacefully, enjoy drinking from their bottles, and are both healthy, fresh, lively, good looking, and will make their way with confidence, while their mother still has to ponder what life is all about.

Else described the return trip to Wistaria. She travelled by train from Hazelton to Burns Lake, noting that "A noisy hockey team got on board in Smithers and created a rumpus until 7 in the morning, when we stopped in Burns Lake."

Once again she stayed at Henkel's lodge:

> Verne Taylor took me to Mrs. Henkel who had prepared everything to be warm and welcoming. François Lake was not safe. Since the temperature went below zero the following night, Johnny Keefe came with a small sleigh and took us safely across the lake. A few times the horse shied away from areas that didn't seem safe, but we arrived safely in Southbank on the other shore. So I was back at Mrs. Keefe's with all her children. I felt I couldn't eat much, since they had only little food for themselves. The hotel was not doing well. Nobody was coming and they did all the work themselves...
>
> The next day, on Sunday at noon, we listened to a radio show from New York. Brüning [Heinrich Brüning, Chancellor of Germany] talked about disarmament. He spoke in English, while I had been looking forward so much to hearing German! ...
>
> Towards evening Dunc McGibbon came with his car and took me to Ootsa, which took an hour. Around midnight, when we were right on the Ootsa Lake, a strong snow storm hit us and quickly created high drifts, so that Dunc had to get out of the car and shovel a path for us. The lights were blinding us. We could barely see anything and lost sight of the shore. For a moment I got scared, when I felt that Dunc was becoming uncertain what to do. Then we saw a light: Ed H.'s house! (They had seen our lights far out there in the storm and had come up with the great idea to put a light in their window). Dunc managed to force the car up to the house where we stopped in front of the door. The storm was howling and reached for me as I

staggered through the knee-deep snow to our house. This is how Gloria came home.

Georg had not heard us coming, as the storm had swallowed up all sounds. Then he was eager and happy to hold his child, which was just 14 days old, on his knees, and Dunc, the bachelor, looked upon this idyllic family scene.

Home at Wistaria, Else was concerned about their financial situation.

Now we have a thousand things to worry about. We have to pay $100 to the hospital and we owe the storekeeper $100 for months now. Georg is away hunting for 4 weeks now but the weather is bad and whatever he will bring home it won't be enough. My mother has more than we do. She sends everything now for the children except for shoes for Rupert which we buy here. I myself wear my old clothes, I am lucky that I have so much that is made from good material to last for years.

Else described a special event that showed the spirit of the community.

I had been back for no longer than a week when all the neighbours came by for a surprise party. All of a sudden, around 8 p.m. the door opened and one after the other filed in, followed by the music. It was awesome. I had not expected this and my mouth fell open. They all took great pleasure in the expression on my face.

The living room was cleared, the linoleum rolled up and a pound of starch sprinkled on the floor. The musicians, who had brought a violin, a guitar and a harmonica, positioned themselves in a corner and the dancing started, to continue until 6 a.m. Around midnight a pound of coffee was poured into the two biggest pots that were then put on the fire. The women had brought cake and sandwiches and we had a nice "supper."

That's what they did this winter, going to all the neighbours in turn, saving money this way and still had fun, even though nobody had a cent! Everyone is in debt, owing the store not only 100 dollars, but a few hundred—and still everybody lives without worrying.

I am not able to do that. I have too much of "Prussian upbringing" in my bones. I am brooding over what I could do. Writing. But 2 children, 2 or 1 ½ babies, 3 beavers, one

> cow, house and farm—when is there time to write? There is just enough time to write some letters or to read a bit, even though that means I have to stay up until midnight and don't get enough sleep. And still, this night I dreamed of Norman: he wore a grass green jacket and I was in love with him; material for a nice short story!

Else's next diary entry was almost four months later, in mid-July. "Today I have to push myself to write in my diary." She expressed her concerns.

> Gloria is smiling and thriving. She is a little sunshine, warm and radiant and the only solace that I can hold tight. We are getting more and more into debt. The furs are on their way to Seattle but not yet sold, and they won't sell for much anyway, as the world revolution is marching without furs. All right. We eat potatoes and onions. When Georg shoots something we eat meat. That is all. I know that many people don't even have that. I sit inside my four walls for days, weeks, months... Everything becomes fuzzy and distant. The pendulum of the small clock marks the daily work; that is all. I cannot write any more. I don't write letters any more. What I write is not

Else and Gloria outside the Seel home. University of Victoria Archives 4-6-43

> true anyway, and writing a diary seems pointless. But where should it go? It is still flowing after all, rising from the heart and glowing in the eyes.

Else wrote about the progress of their beaver farm.

> Georg brought 2 beavers. One of them had lost a front paw, and the other one a webbed hind paw in the trap. This is the 2nd or 3rd time that we lost beavers to this type of injury. The Indian Jimmy Andrews brought 2 more animals: a pregnant female who gave birth to 2 dead pups and a little later had 2 live pups. Our first one, Eva, also had pups; we don't know how many, since she won't leave the nest that she made.
>
> Last Sunday a well built and educated Indian came in his nice car and brought a box with 2 one-month-old beavers. They were really cute and I couldn't resist buying them for 5 dollars each. It was a pair, and I named the male beaver "Billy" and the female "Dolly." We put an extra house into the pen and I was worried that the other beavers would bite them. But George, the Indian from New Hazelton, said I shouldn't worry. He carefully wrote down his address and left. The next morning, when I checked on them, Billy and Dolly were unharmed and came towards me. I took Billy inside the house with me. He explored all the corners, ate, drank milk, and built himself a nest from a rag behind the stove in the kitchen, gnawed on my straw broom and the firewood box, and slept peacefully until I put him back into the pen. The next morning both of them had disappeared and I didn't know if they had been adopted or if something else had happened. So now we have 6 old beavers and 6 young ones and are running out of space.

For Dominion Day, the Seel family had visitors: "Kurt U. appeared again as chauffeur for Mrs. Keefe and Mikosch, a man from Styria who he had picked up in Burns [Lake]. He talked in an Austrian dialect and sang 'In einem kühlen Grunde' " ["In a cool valley," a poem by German Romantic poet, Joseph von Eichendorff, set to music by Johann Glück].

The community held their annual picnic, which Else described.

> There was a picnic but everything was quiet and subdued; nobody seemed to be in a good mood, even though there were piles of cake and ice cream. The times leave a mark on the

> people here too. In the evening there was a dance, but it was not as much fun as usual. When we got home at 3 o'clock in the morning Georg and Mr. Henkel, who had arrived 2 days ago, had just finished with their maps and Klondike stories and had gone to bed. The next morning we had a long breakfast... They sang a few songs, took some photographs, and off they went.

At the end of her entry Else wrote: "Georg will be away for 10 days and I will be alone, as always. I milk Tynee who has a calf, the little Tillie. We want to keep her as a second dairy cow because the children need milk—a lot of milk. We also eat potatoes and onions and rhubarb from the garden, that's more than enough."

George spent the summer prospecting in the Tahtsa drainage. In early September Else described his unsuccessful venture.

> One week ago Georg came home, beaming: "I found it!" He had been looking at Placer Creek for 2 months, trying to find out where the gold came from that showed up in the creek. Up and down the creek he had panned for gold, had found a black rock with gold particles in it and thought he had found something promising when there was a wide rim of gold dust in his pan. I had to type half a dozen letters and said "I don't believe that fate favours us like this," and it didn't. Old Bill who had been with Georg just brought the news: "fool's gold." I couldn't eat anything for the rest of the day and was wondering if the store would still give us credit. Poor Georg, he works all the time but can't make a cent.

The same month Copp wrote a letter from Trout Lake (a mining area in the West Kootenay district), probably in response to George's prospecting activities.

> Your letter of the 26th of August just reached me today and needless to say I was pleased to hear from you. I left Vancouver on the 29th to come up here and open up some old tunnels so that they could sample the property. I do not know how long I will be here. I have written to my wife to have the samples sent to the assay office and when I get the results I will forward them to you. I will send you the number of my miner's license and if by chance you should have the chance I would like for you to stake a claim for me.

> I was in Alaska when your letter came over a year ago and when I got back I just could not get down to answer it... I am at present doing this work for a big operation company and if your claims stand up I can interest them, they are in the market for gold property. If you are home write me upon receipt of this and give me as much of a description of the claims as possible. Have you any quartz?

Copp wrote another letter in late October that confirmed George had not found gold.

> I have just returned from the Kootenay and seen Capt. Irving who has just returned from a trip to the Yukon by airplane. I had him send your samples to Victoria. I am enclosing the certificate. Sorry to see that it did not run. I cannot understand how the gold came to be here that you panned. It seems hard to get anything that will stand up for sampling. Things are very quiet here just now, there is some inquiries for gold properties.
>
> Hoping to hear from you soon again and trusting this finds you and the family in the best of health.

On her birthday in November, Else wrote in her diary, describing the physical and psychological effects of the Depression.

> My birthday. I couldn't bake a cake because I had no milk, butter or eggs. Tynee didn't find any food and dried up. Georg is gone, chasing gold. He said: "Let the cow run loose when she doesn't give any milk" and that's what I did. I drink black coffee, or rather brown water. Only once a week I take a handful of coffee for a fresh brew. I have bread with it that I roast in a pan. It is ok. We also have game meat. The same food for over a year now. For salt and as a side dish: loneliness and worries and nice letters of people asking for money. The distress of our times. There is some evaporated milk left for the children but what to do when that is gone? Mother sent me a few dollars that I used to buy flour and lard and gasoline. Georg took all of it with him. Is he a fool or am I?
>
> I cannot write any more, not even letters. Why should I bother other people with my worries? Everyone has their own problems. I have to stay here because of the children, otherwise I would have left long ago to make a living somewhere else.

Else's next diary entry was almost three months later, at the end of January 1933. Her main thoughts were still about coping with conditions during the Depression.

> Life creeps on. Georg is always gone. At least he is hunting so that he will bring something home. Until Christmas he was looking for gold, without any success.
>
> In the evenings or half the night I read, English and German newspapers and magazines so that I don't have to think. We still didn't pay off our debts. Last year's income was a total of $69.50 from furs that were sold in Seattle. It cannot get worse this year. The other men work for one week once a month on the road and get $15–20. It's called relief work and offered by the government like a handout. Georg would feel terrible to do this and as long as my mother helps us we are ok. I didn't have any new stockings or clothes for the past 2 years. I mend and sew all the time.

Trapping was more productive that winter. In mid-March, Else noted: "Georg came back at the end of February with a good catch: 9 marten and a mink. Half went to Norman [Schreiber] for flour and butter. The 4 best furs were sent for auction in Montreal. Georg chopped wood for one week and then left again."

In Else's next entry, on June 20, she wrote about the first family outing that they had taken in several months. Early in the month they went by boat to visit the Mohr family, who had finished building a new house. A storm occurred on the return trip and the waves were high enough to splash into the boat and soak the children. They pulled into the bay below the Ed Harrison house. The Harrisons were home, so the Seel family got dry and warmed up before walking home in a snowstorm.

Else wrote about more financial difficulties. Their milk cow died, "So we have now lost the cow that provided us with food all of last summer. Now old Mrs. H. gives us one liter of milk a day and one pound of butter a week which is not enough for cooking and baking and it costs us 5 dollars a month that we don't have."

Trapping in the latter part of the winter was not as successful: "Georg brought only a few pelts that were of bad quality, just enough to pay the store bill. Now we have to live on credit until winter. That is half the money we make even though we buy only the essentials. Last month I didn't order anything, not even for a cent. We eat bread, potatoes and the eggs from our chickens. The children drink the milk."

They planted a large garden to produce more food. Else wrote that "It grows well and we should have enough for next year. We sowed a sack of potatoes and big packets of German seeds."

They obtained two more beavers, including a female who had three pups. Else noted that feeding them was a lot of work.

Adolf Hitler was appointed chancellor of Germany in January 1933, and his Nazi party won the most seats in the election that March. Else was following events in Germany and commented: "Adolf Hitler brings everything under government control in Germany. I wonder what will grow out of this mess. First of all, books are burnt... and all the Jews are chased away and their jobs are taken by more or less Christian people... I am glad that I am not in Germany. I would have the same opposition as during and after the war, but I am not as passionate any more. I'd rather sing children's songs."

In late August, Else noted that they were having a good harvest: "There is more hay than in the past 10 years and lots of wheat, oats and potatoes." Pearl and Charlie Henson opened a store in Wistaria. Now the people along the western end of Ootsa Lake wouldn't have to travel so far for supplies. "Georg built the chimney and got 15 dollars credit for it. We danced all night until 6 in the morning to celebrate the opening. When I went home by myself a bear family made noise in the bushes by the path but I felt safer than in Berlin at this time of day." Unfortunately, Charlie died in an accident that December.

George helped the Mohrs making hay, and in return "They lent us a cow that gives barely one liter of milk a day. Her name, 'Queen', is a bit pretentious, but she saves us 10 cents a day which is a lot. The price for wheat rose

Else in a boat with Gloria and Rupert. University of Victoria Archives 4-6-45

rapidly last month, just to drop again just as quickly. Furs are good so far. At least we manage to crawl little by little out of our debt-hole. We can live without getting more into debt, even though it means living frugally."

In 1933, 1935, 1938 and 1939, Else kept a small pocketbook diary. She used this to make a brief (usually one or two lines) record of daily events. The pocketbook diaries show the interaction with other residents of the area; how they assisted each other; and visited neighbours where coffee, dessert and conversation were always provided. The Seel family's contact with First Nations people is also documented. The 1933 diary contained several references to visits from First Nations people, particularly Jimmy Andrews. In late March, "Jimmy Andrews and Robert Skin get boards for coffin for 19 year old Indian woman." In early April, Jimmy and three other First Nations people stopped to visit. A few days later, "Indian woman Mary barters pillow case for dress and pyjamas." The next day, "Robert Skin and family bring moccasins." Towards the end of the month, Jimmy Andrews stopped by again and played the fiddle.

Else recorded that a group of First Nations people camped at their property in mid-June, but left after a big argument among themselves. In early August, "the Indians Skin barter leather bags for linen." The next day Mrs. Andrews brought moccasins for Rupert and Gloria, followed two days

Jimmy Andrews playing the fiddle. Else Seel photograph. University of Victoria Archives 4-3-23

later by Jimmy, who brought meat. Late in the month, the Skin family visited again. In September, Andrews came and brought moccasins.

In her pocket diary Else noted celebrating New Year's at the Mohrs' household from midnight to 3:00 am. George left for trapping a few days later, and on January 7 Bob Nelson came in the snow to bring the mail and open the water hole on the lake, which had frozen in the cold weather. During that winter, when Rupert was four and Gloria had her first birthday, it was difficult for Else to leave the house, so the neighbours often brought the mail while George was away. Some also brought food, particularly butter.

Else took her first trip to the Tahtsa River in September. The children stayed with neighbours, while she and George spent five days visiting the area where his trapline and abandoned mine were located. Since this was a special trip, Else recorded it in detail in a separate account. She also took her camera.

TAHTSA RIVER

by Else Lübcke-Seel

Placer Creek on Tahtsa River, September 19, 1933

The camp fire is burning. I am lying in the tent in the wilderness of the Canadian Pacific Mountains, writing.

This morning we left our log cabin in Wistaria in pouring rain. Ootsa Lake was calm until after 8 miles [12km] we reached Windy Point, which indeed was windy. But since we had the wind in the back we could tolerate it well, while an Indian boat coming towards us swayed up and down heavily. The woman, wearing a red headscarf, lifted her right arm, which is the usual salute out here.

We get to the end of Ootsa Lake. The green Tahtsa is clearly visible. Wide and calm, it flows into the lake. We tootle away under a now clearer sky and dull sun. Willow bushes are hanging into the water on the right and left; behind them meadows and knolls, and hills with deciduous and coniferous forests.

At the forks the wide Tahtsa River divides and lets the Whitesail join its bed. We go up our loyal Tahtsa River that gives us berries and fish in the summer, moose, deer, goats and bears in the fall, the valuable furs of the fur-bearing animals in winter and then finally in spring beavers and muskrats for our farm.

At noon we drink tea under high fir and spruce trees. There are large meadows full of swamp grasses here that the farmers from Wistaria get to feed their cows during the winter when the hay harvest is scarce, like last year when the winter lasted 8 months and brought weeks of cold temperatures between 50 and 70 degrees. Cattle died in droves. Our neighbour lost 22 dairy cows and a dozen calves. He himself broke through the ice with his sled and could jump off just in time to save his life. Horses and sled disappeared under the ice. In the spring Georg cut the harnesses off the dead horses and also pulled blankets and forks out of the water. Fate can be cruel out here but nobody seems to get too affected. The people here have this old pioneering spirit without which the loneliness and hard labour could barely be endured. [During the cold winter Bob Nelson took his horses to the meadows at the west end of Ootsa Lake because his supply of hay was gone. The slough grass provided food, although it did not have much nutrition. On the return trip, the animals broke through the ice and drowned. Else recorded this event in March when Jimmy Andrews visited and brought the information.]

Gradually the water starts to flow faster. The river banks come closer and masses of rocks, covered in moss close in, with spruce and pines sticking out like needles in a pin cushion.

Mile by mile the small outboard motor brings us uphill. I dip the paddle in the water to measure the speed and it is almost knocked out of my hand: here the Tahtsa runs at 8 miles per hour.

Now and then the water is shallow. September brings the lowest water level of the year. We pass the tent of the water measurers who are employed by the government and measure the changing water levels of the Tahtsa River. The meter is a ticking in a small wooden hut; a clock, wound up once a month stipples the information on a constantly revolving paper roll.

Once we have to get out of the boat to pull it around a shallow edge. There are beaver tracks in the damp sand on the shore. How well I know those.

We travel 32 miles [50 kilometres] up the river. That is enough for one day. We pitch the tent under the balsams. Bacon and eggs sizzle over the open fire and the coffee is boiling. It tastes delicious. Evening comes quickly. It is raining again and the owls are crying and go out hunting. Good night, Tahtsa!

Tahtsa Mining Cabin, September 20, 1933

Unlike I had expected, no bears came during the night to steal the bacon from our provisions box, and no moose or deer crashed through the forest. Only muskrats splashed at the river bank and plopped into the water, and a curious squirrel slipped through a hole in the tent canvas and examined everything, rattling through plates and lids and rustling with paper.

We woke from the "honk, honk" sounds of wild geese. They flew past us so closely that I heard the swooshing of their wings. A little way further off they swooped down into the water and noisily took their morning bath.

It was still dawn. Fog wavered above the river. We quickly packed our things, put them in the boat and off we went. Along the shores grew gigantic balsams, as high as apartment buildings in a big city; they stood bolt upright, one next to the other, forming a majestic road.

It got lighter and lighter. The fog sailed away, leaving behind only a few hovering, delicate veils. The dark green water barely moved; here and there white down feathers floated on the surface. Then the sun came through and the landscape glowed in the silence. It was indescribably beautiful. An eagle comes from the mountains and flies silently high above us.

We turn off the engine and Georg pushes the boat forward with a long pole. The Tahtsa gets wider and wider. The green walls on both sides turn into a grand bend and open up to a vast plain with snow peaked mountains in the background. Birds singing and flitting through the air above man-high grasses, red flower spikes, and fall-coloured willow bushes. Ducks rise clumsily and flocks of wild geese migrate above us. A kingfisher darts around. Fresh moose tracks, massive like the tracks of a heavy bull, are dug into the sand at the riverbank. Magical moments in an almost untouched wilderness.

We have a long way ahead of us and the engine has to do its duty again. Bend by bend we meander through these magical meadows into which canals branch off everywhere. We cut off the path of a mink that cheekily wants to cross in front of us, but he dives quickly and comes back to the surface again far away from us.

A view of Tahtsa River from the Copp cabin. Else Seel photograph. University of Victoria Archives 4-6-39

Else at the Copp mining cabin. University of Victoria Archives 4-6-39

The sun disappears. First a few drops fall and then it starts to rain more and more. The bed of the Tahtsa gets wider once again. The wall of green firs appears again on both sides and we disembark at the first trapper cabin.

This is where the realm of the trappers starts. Those men follow the frozen rivers and lakes during the winter, cross the mountains and stomp hundreds of miles through meter deep snow on broad, plate-like snow shoes that they braid themselves from moose skin. With bodies and muscles like steel they seem like the last heroes that undermine civilization. There are about half a dozen of those trappers here that have mastered this trade for the past 10 or 20 years. There are barely any trainees; it is beyond the strength of the young people to endure the hardships and the months of loneliness in the mountains. A trapper's cabin is made from raw logs, forming a square big enough to hold a plank bed, a camping stove, and a box with a board attached to it to serve as a chair and table. The door is a window through which one enters since the snow often covers the entire hut. The pointed roof is made from halved logs and makes the small room just man-high in the middle; in all the other places of the cabin one has to stoop in order to not hit the ceiling. In those dingy cabins hung thousands of dollars worth of furs: marten, mink, ermine, silver, red and grey foxes, wolves, coyotes, otters, lynx and beavers. Today the trappers barely make a living. Licenses and taxes on every fur and expenses for provisions and equipment eat up most of the income that is hard to earn considering the low fur prices.

Mile by mile we ride the old Tahtsa. It gets colder, the mountains come in closer and the river banks become steeper. Here and there floodwaters uprooted trees and bushes that now protrude into the river or are stacked sideways.

In the afternoon we finally stop. Here at the mountainside is Georg's cabin, the "home cabin," one of 21 that are scattered along the trapping line but in most cases are only logs leaning against each other like a roof, so that the smoke from the fire can rise like through an open tent.

Soon we cook beans and bacon on the small stove. I rummage around old tobacco and tin cans, discover a suitcase under the bed, as well as magazines, mittens and bear furs, everything gnawed on by rats. Since there is a broom I sweep. Sitting on the box and the bed we eat our meal which is warming and tastes delicious. Than we wash our dishes, clean up and on we go.

We turn to leave the Tahtsa and get to a branch directly at the foot of the mountain where our silver mine used to be. The mining cabin is still there. It is quite roomy, with a stove and cooking utensils. We unload our things and want to stay here overnight. We walk up the path to the mine. Big logs fell across the path in the three years since the mine was given up. Pack horses loaded with sacks and boxes used to climb this path every day. Georg shows me a gold vein, but it is too small to exploit. We reach the mine. The tunnel is covered in snow and the cabin burnt down except for the powder house, sad remnants of a proud hope. If the world market value of silver increases again one day, perhaps the mine will start working again.

Consolidated Mining Cabin, September 21 and 22, 1933

Today we stay here. This is the second dead mine in the land. It was called the "Emerald Mine." but I am sure it did not produce any precious stones

Emerald Landing on the north side of the Tahtsa River. Else Seel photograph. University of Victoria Archives 3-33-12

for the Consolidated Mining and Smelting Company. The company worked here for three years with 20 to 30 people on average, dragging in all provisions, tractors and compressors, Archimedean and steel drills 65 miles [105 kilometres] across the land and 70 miles [112 kilometres] on the water, then 8 miles [12 kilometres] up the mountain. They paid the workers 150–200 dollars per month and provided free and ample food. I find a box full of old papers: pay sheets from the years 29 and 30, reports from the mining engineers to the company, invoices from department stores in Vancouver, from merchants in Prince Rupert and Burns Lake, freight certificates of Canadian National, invoices from the truck driver and the hotels for the workers, telegrams in which the engineer asks for more workers and the respective reply telegrams stating that no more mining workers can be recruited; not only once, but six times, with different dates, a mockery in the year 1933! The biggest mining company in Canada spent half a million for nothing. They found only small ore deposits even though the diamond drill had been driven criss-cross through the mountain.

Here is the most dangerous part of the Tahtsa. It roars and tumbles, frothing white and piling up large trees with their roots pointing upwards. We laboriously make our way uphill. The river bed keeps on getting narrower. The rocks on the sides are cracked and cleaved, forming bizarre rock arches.

At a sharp bend we get out and visit the grave of Bill Grell... a painter and railway robber who drowned here. I once saw one of his paintings in a farmhouse: Indians stoning a bear. They push heavy boulders onto a bear that is trapped in a ravine... A mighty rock arch appears and we speed through it. The cabin sits right on the river bank with the mighty mountain rising behind it.

We disembark and have supper. Three beds with mattresses are still there and we sleep very well with the sound of the Tahtsa rushing in the background. When I woke up the next morning I said drowsily: "Georg, it is raining!" but it was the Tahtsa rushing and burbling outside.

We climb up the mountain. Now it is really raining. Water is dripping from the blue spruces. Clusters of red berries like mountain ash shine through the green. There are birch trees and poplars and white lichens on the ground. The higher we get the greater the view becomes despite the gloomy weather. Lakes are scattered among the meadows. Far below us the Tahtsa winds itself in meanders around the mountain.

Slowly the magnificent trees disappear. The snow that we had seen shimmering for a while comes closer. There are the mountains. A strange and ragged mountain range is called "The Rhine Stones," named by a Canadian surveyor who had been at the Rhine during the world war. [Rhine Crag was named by Frank Swannell, who surveyed on this peak in 1921.]

In pouring rain we climb down the mountain on the other side and get to Tahtsa Lake, an elongated, 65 mile [105 kilometres] long lake. This is where the Tahtsa originates, making its way in a big arch through British Columbia, separated from the Pacific only by a narrow mountain range and finally flowing into the ocean through the Fraser River near Vancouver.

We walk through the virgin forest on moose and bear trails. It is dark and eerily quiet. No sound. Georg walks ahead with the carbine. Often we have to climb laboriously over dead tree trunks. At one time something crashes through the thickets on the side: an animal taking flight. I wish I could experience seeing an animal but it does not show itself. Only the rain is drumming onto the forest canopy, though no drops get to us. Curious squirrels dart up and down the trees and rail at us terribly. When the forest starts to thin out a great hawk swoops down on my green cap. For a moment he is so close that I scream. Georg of course is laughing. And while I believe to still be deep in the forest the cabin is already in sight again.

Wistaria, September 23, 1933

The next morning we speed down the Tahtsa, floating downhill without stop. We are whizzing past the trapper cabins and the now familiar shores at the speed of an express train until we stop at the meadow paradise to get a goose for the pot. However, an eagle that had followed us for miles flew ahead and was waiting for us on a tree, angrily lamenting and cawing with odd high-pitched sounds. He then flew on and continued to stay close to our boat. When Georg disembarked to sneak up on the geese the eagle flew ahead and alarmed them with his wild screeches. Gabbling, they soared in large flocks and flew towards the mountains.

Thus we floated down the good Tahtsa. We met tourists from Mexico who travelled comfortably in three boats with two guides, a servant and a cook. They wanted to hunt bears and asked Georg lots of questions and he gave them lots of answers.

This time we got shaken about quite a bit at Windy Point but I remained stoic, knowing that our house was on the opposite shore. There it was, nestled close to the shore of Ootsa Lake and the children came running outside to greet us.

On December 8, Else wrote a detailed diary entry that contained a lengthy description about the death and burial of Charlie Henson. She also commented: "I am alone again for over a month now. I don't get as upset any more.

The children are good company now." Later in this entry she wrote: "This winter is mild. Georg brought already 4 minks that were sold to Charlie Henson for $6.50. I sent the best ones to Spencer in Vancouver and got only $6, how strange. At least I could order coffee, nuts, and ingredients for cake so that Rupert can celebrate his 5th birthday."

Else also described the kindness of one of her neighbours to Rupert, who "gets our liter of milk every morning that the good old Mrs. Harrison gives us so generously! She has raised 12 children, all the H.'s right and left of us... She knows well what it's like to be poor and she silently stretched out her kind hand and helped us a bit."

In late January 1934, Else wrote about events that had occurred during the past six weeks: "Mid-December it started snowing and didn't stop until Christmas. Old Bill came by horse to bring milk, and only the neck of the horse peeked out of the snow! I worked hard feeding the beavers. The snow went up to my hips, I shoveled snow away from the dens and doors, carried poplar branches, getting sweaty and falling face down into the snow several times. Tears ran down my face and froze. What a woman can bear when she has to!"

George returned home from trapping two days before Rupert's birthday, bringing a few more furs.

> He brought only 2 martens and 4 mink. We had to send them away for sale quickly in order to pay at least our fire insurance, since we had lived in an uninsured house for 3 months.
>
> Then the temperatures dropped to 40-50 below zero! Everyone stayed home by the oven, and we didn't see anybody. But then on Rupert's birthday 15 people showed up, half of them children. We had cake and candy and a bright Christmas tree, and we sang and played.
>
> I received the first $20 from my inheritance and could pay for milk and butter for 3 months, buy a turkey, and some necessary things for Georg.

She also commented on the situation in Germany: "I received some photographs of my cousins, all with swastika armbands, even the ones that were just schoolboys. Everyone raves about renewal and is keen on war and action. The apple rolls between white and red, white and red." [This refers to the novel *Little Apple* by the Austrian writer Leo Perutz. The title of his novel became a buzzword at the end of the 1920s, expressing fears and uncertainty about the future of the people at that time]. Else concluded by writing: "Long live the Tahtsa River!"

Else only made one diary entry between January and July, and it was mainly about the death of her German friend, Kurt Unger.

Economic conditions improved in 1934. In the summer Else wrote: "In June Georg had work for 2 weeks, the first time in 3 years, cleaning up the Tahtsa River. For the $50 we could pay the provisions for the past 3 months." Bill McNeill received a federal government contract to clear the log-jams out of the Tahtsa River to make it safe for travel. McNeill hired George since he knew the river and was experienced in using dynamite.

The two men continued working during the summer: "Georg is with McNeill at Placer Lake, digging and blasting holes to get samples. Everyone is excited about gold. Mines spring up like mushrooms. People spend money again and the dollar is rising—prosperity is around the corner."

George and Else's garden produced a large quantity of food: "The Indian Summer brought two to three warm days, the rest were windy and rainy. The harvest was good. Eight hundredweights [370 kilograms] potatoes despite the frost, 20 hundredweights [910 kilograms] carrots and three tons [1360 kilograms] of rutabagas that will feed the cow. Yesterday we cut up cabbages and made a barrel of sauerkraut."

However, not everything was positive, as Else wrote in mid-October.

> Georg was sick with rheumatism for 6 weeks. He lay on the couch a lot and was listless and restless. Since then we sleep in separate beds; he stays on the couch. We now have public work here, $15 per month to pay for flour and sugar at the store after having toiled so much for 3 years. Trapping has become useless but Georg still wants to get over his trapping line one more time to earn the money for his clothes. Mother in Berlin still looks after the children even though sending money is now forbidden.
>
> Anyway, we are alive and the hard times will pass. The days are filled with work and meaning and the children grow and make me happy—that's how it should be.

Usually George was at his trapline on Else's birthday, and it was often a quiet day for her. But her fortieth birthday was a special event.

> On my birthday I went to the post office. The path was muddy and I got wet and cold. I stopped at the Nelson's, took off my shoes and warmed my feet by Mrs. Nelson's oven, and chatted with everybody until it got dark. A feeling told me: "today will be special for you" and look: I got a long, lovely letter from J. M. Frank the author of "The last four from St. Paul" that I had liked so much that I had written him a few lines. He had also

> sent a package with books: a copy of the "Last four," "Don't be afraid of Tomorrow" and "The man who loved Greta Garbo." [Josef Maria Frank was a German writer and screenwriter.] I took all the books and walked back home through the mud and dirt, singing. Half way I saw a lantern. It was Georg who was worried that I got lost. A rare sign of love from him. It was the happiest moment of the entire year.
>
> Georg got healthy again and was happy as always. He worked on the road for 6 weeks which is called public work and is a kind of relief. A week ago he went trapping again.

In early February 1935, Else wrote about Christmas and the cold weather they had that winter.

> Another new year, this time with 60 below zero. Everything was frozen. All my flowers froze except a few hyacinth bulbs, that are now starting to bloom. I took them inside, closed my eyes and inhaled their scent. I am happy despite my poor and modest way of life.
>
> Rupert turned 6 years old and Gloria is now 3. They start to walk by themselves for short distances. At Christmas Santa Claus came to the Hall and to our house, bringing packages from Omi [grandmother] from Berlin. We had slaughtered a pig, made liver sausage and head cheese, and had made a barrel of sauerkraut. Good food for the first time in years. Kind letters came in the mail, and picture books, other books, a German newspaper with a lot of hallelujah; should one believe that?... Only J. M. Frank, being a poet, is high above everything on his Pegasus and set his mind to writing "The people of Wistaria" and in order to do that he wants to come here with his wife Irene, if he gets the foreign currency. But why should it work out? It would be too good to be true.
>
> Somehow the light shines a bit brighter again. Georg has been away for 2 weeks now. I hope he will bring a few furs so I can go to Smithers to see the dentist. I haven't been away for weeks, except walking over to the beavers on snow shoes to feed them.
>
> Nothing is happening here. Rarely a sled comes across the lake, when the Harrison's visit each other. François Lake is frozen and Mrs. Henkel wrote that she never felt so out of the way

> as here in the interior of B.C. It's true, it is a bit too lonely here and I lose my sense of time, but my Pomeranian stoicism helps me to get through that.

George returned later in the month "with a fisher that we sold for $50. We could pay all our food, even the thought of that is like a little celebration. Then there was the Valentine's dance, organized by the C.C.F. Club. It was founded by half a dozen people on January 9 by Ed Mohr and consists mainly of the Harrisons, and myself. It will take a while for the C.C.F. but people are discontented with the two old parties and at every meeting there are a few more members." [The Co-operative Commonwealth Federation, formed in 1932, was the forerunner of the New Democratic Party. The CCF ran candidates in the 1935 federal election.]

In early March, Else recorded a visit from Baptiste and two of his children, who brought moccasins for Rupert and Gloria. Later that month, Else and Baptiste's wife went to Buster Harrison's place for a visit. In mid-April, Mrs. Baptiste and some friends stopped at the house.

Else wrote about several events in her April 28 entry:

"Today is Rupert's first day of school. At 8 a.m. he left with the 8-year-old Ernie Harrison in a snow flurry. Georg had already left at 4 am to hunt some muskrats. I fed the cow who came back two days ago looking like a skeleton and has just enough milk for her calf."

The Franks still planned to come to Wistaria: "Irene Frank, the wife of Josef Maria... wrote two kind letters, asking what she should wear over here and what she should bring. They are thinking about travelling to Vancouver via the Panama Canal. It would be nice, very nice if they could come." Unfortunately for Else, the trip did not occur.

There were some improvements to the house: "Our kitchen is painted pink and I hung up new curtains. It's the first time after 5 years that we have a few dollars for renovation."

In the spring, George received an inquiry from Robert McComb of Juneau, Alaska, about selling his mine. McComb was involved in mining ventures in that state. In a telegram on May 8, George replied: "Property for sale. Wait for letter with instructions." George described the situation in his reply on May 14.

> Received a telegram from you stating the British Columbia Stock Comp. would like to handle my property. I have already wired you that I am ready for a deal.
>
> The reason they have stopped working 1930 was the low price of silver, also the tumbling down of oil stock, which you

> know, was their main income. There is 300 feet [90 metres] tunnel, making ore for 100 feet [30 metres] of very good grade, also some surface work has been done exposing ore at different points; very little work is needed to start mining again.
>
> It is not advisable to have a man look at the showing till first part of June on account of the late spring we are having this year. Any details of the property the Company wants they might find them at the government office in Victoria as Douglas Lay, resident engineer, has examined twice. If your Comp[any] want to take hold of, just have them correspond with me.
>
> Many thanks for your kindness and if there is any money in it for me you will not have to do it for nothing. Trusting I see you again on Ootsa Lake someday.

George's hopes of selling the mine never materialized.

During the summer George worked for much of the time. Else wrote on August 10: "Summer is almost over. Georg was always away, first bridge

Rupert and Gloria in the garden. Else Seel photograph. University of Victoria Archives 4-6-45

construction and then transporting parts from the mine. The Consolidated Company is dismantling everything and takes all their equipment from the mine."

Else recorded in her diary on October 21: "A beautiful long fall. Georg is on his last freight tour and made $300. Almost all of that went into paying off our debts. Even the store bill is paid and it feels a bit lighter." She wrote that "Twice I went by boat on the Ootsa Lake, my only time away."

Her next entry was not until February 26, 1936.

> Everything passes so quickly. The fall was over, then winter came with a bit of snow and Christmas with a small radio, the first present in years... I got news that mother is very ill and lying in a hospital in Schöneberg, but she picked herself up and would like me to come next winter...
>
> On January 28 was Gloria's birthday and Carry's wedding [Caroline McNeill, Bill McNeill's daughter]. We went with Old Harrisons by sleigh to Ootsa. It took us 4 hours and we were quite stiff when we arrived. For the first time in 5 years I had put on a new black taffeta dress, and at 1 p.m. Jack Knox and Carry got married under an arch made of snow shoes. 60 people from all around the Ootsa Lake attended. Then we went home again after briefly stopping at Schreiber's...
>
> Georg has been away trapping for one month now. It was the worst month of the whole winter. Continuous cold of 40 to 50, and even 60 below zero. It was terrible, like being in an ice cave. My breath froze even when sitting next to the oven! And I was alone and sick with swollen tonsils and a horrible ear ache, until finally one ear burst and it got better. All our potatoes and all the vegetables in the root house were frozen even though we had put a lamp in there. The "Old Hinsche" came for 4 days and even though he is deaf and clumsy it was very comforting to have him around. [Hinsche, also known as Hephata, was originally from Germany. He had worked as a gaucho in Argentina and on a farm in the Prairies before coming to the Ootsa area in the mid-1930s and settling at Streatham. Hinsche, who was deaf and communicated by writing, visited the Seel residence occasionally.]

In October, Else described the summer:

> Summer came and went quickly, with the first snow at the beginning of September. Nonetheless we had a good harvest. The first strawberries grew on our berry patch and we harvested currants from the bushes we had planted 3 years ago as cuttings from François Lake.
>
> Georg had a bit of work, just enough to get by, and the cow and the chickens contributed too. Rupert started grade 2 and Gloria grows like a flower. We were away twice on the boat, and visited Hephata amongst his illustrated bibles and paper windows, and with nothing in the house but a bit of ground wheat...

Else wrote about the frustrations of accessing the inheritance money that she had in Germany: “Since the spring I try to get the money to go to Berlin, but with no success. The Exchange Control Office didn’t approve anything, not even travelling on German ships. So Aunt Emma paid for the entire trip Prince Rupert–Hamburg and back and I will probably leave next month.”

In 1936 and 1937 Paddy and Beatrice (Sammie) Carroll took a trip across North America with their dog team. They reached Halifax and New York before returning to Wistaria. Else took this photograph of the Carrolls with their dog team outside their home on Ootsa Lake. University of Victoria Archives 3-32-5

When there was no snow, the Carrolls devised a wheeled structure with three motorcycle wheels to fit around their dog sled. The dogs are taking a rest on their epic trip. The sign says "Trans Canada Dog Team." University of Victoria Archives 3-35-6

Else left by herself in late October. Much of her time in Germany was spent helping her mother pack and clean out her apartment in Berlin and then move back to Pomerania, where she took up residence at the house of Else's brother George and his family. During the times that George was away working while Else was in Germany, the children stayed at the homes of various neighbours.

She returned to Burns Lake on July 1. No one was at the train to meet her, but fortunately "Billy Harrison arrives with his truck and takes me home. At the picnic place [the annual Dominion Day event] I can embrace Rupert and Gloria who have grown and are shy. One week later Georg comes back from Tahtsa and the old life starts again." Else brought back a large supply of clothes for the family; an eiderdown sleeping bag for George; and some books.

Else's next entry was in early February 1938: "It's the middle of winter and already a month into the new year. The summer was beautiful, busy, and full of people and sunshine. Every month Georg had a bit of work and made almost 100 dollars each month; he hadn't made that much since 1930."

The main event in the Ootsa area during the summer of 1937 was the visit of the Governor General of Canada. John Buchan, Lord Tweedsmuir, was Governor General from 1935 to 1940. While he held this position, he travelled extensively around the country. In July and early August of 1937, he was the first Governor General to visit the Arctic, travelling from Edmonton to the Arctic Ocean, going by boat down the Mackenzie River. About a week after this trip, Lord Tweedsmuir came to central British Columbia to visit the large, new provincial park that would be named for him in 1938. The *Canadian Alpine Journal* published an article describing both of Lord Tweedsmuir's trips.

> **Lord Tweedsmuir's Visit to Tweedsmuir Park, British Columbia**
>
> On August 15, 1937 Lord Tweedsmuir, then Governor General of Canada, Lady Tweedsmuir and their party visited the region set aside by the British Columbia government as a park and subsequently named Tweedsmuir Park in his honor.
>
> They left the train at Burns Lake, a small town on the Jasper-Rupert branch about 400 miles [644 kilometres] west of Jasper and about 315 miles [500 kilometres] east of Prince Rupert. They travelled by motor car southerly to Ootsa Lake, the northerly boundary of the park, a distance of 42 miles [65 kilometres], crossing on the way François Lake by a Government ferry. On arrival at Ootsa Lake lunch was spent at Ootsa

Lord and Lady Tweedsmuir. T.W.S. Parsons photograph. Parsons was a BC Provincial Police Commissioner who accompanied the Tweedsmuirs during this trip. Royal BC Museum, BC Archives J-00862

Lake Lodge. They were accompanied by the Hon. A. W. Gray, Minister of Lands, Messrs Connally, Kenney, LeBourdais, three men of the British Columbia Legislature, and others. After lunch the party drove about two miles [3 kilometres] along the road adjoining Ootsa Lake to Wilsons Bay, where boats were anchored in a quiet place. The open boats, driven by gasoline power, then sailed down the lake and the rapids in Ootsa River to Camp Susan under the direction of Billy McNeill, an experienced guide of Ootsa. The camp, which had been specially built by the Provincial Government for their guests, was situated in an attractive bay on Intata Lake at the

Getting ready to go fishing. T.W.S. Parsons photograph. Royal BC Museum, BC Archives J-00860

> outlet of Ootsa River, on a height about 20 feet [6 metres] above the water level on a flat bench. Almost every day was spent in fishing and by trips on the water, going as far as the Nechako River. Trips by aeroplane were also taken from day to day as there were several planes available for use. The Great Circle trip taken by tourists by water, covering a distance of about 300 miles [480 kilometres], was made by plane. The fishing was successful and the hospital at Burns Lake as well as the party benefited by the results. After spending several days in this way the party went by plane to Stuie Lodge, now known as Tweedsmuir Lodge.

Bill McNeill, who provided the guiding services, hired George to help him. Else wrote:

> Lord Tweedsmuir was here with his wife and son Alistair to see the park that is named after him. A tent town was erected. Crates of rum and whiskey were brought and fat M.P.'s and other officials who accompanied the party drank and played poker in one of the tents. Georg had built a new boat and took his Excellency fishing. The Scottish writer John Buchan sat there for hours, fishing. Airplanes flew constantly above us. Newspapers published articles of the "Vice Regal Party" and Ootsa Lake was in the limelight for the first time.

The Burns Lake *Advance* described the Governor General's time in the area.

> At Intata Lake, where the party spent several days, a small tent community had risen in the wilderness. For the vice-regal party, attendants and invited guests, thirty or more tents had been erected and they were not altogether without the conveniences to make life enjoyable. Four airplanes were at Intata Lake at the call or fancy of the members of the party, and by this means there were many trips of exploration of the extensive area known as Tweedsmuir Park. There was excellent fishing and boats were provided for this sport, which was taken full advantage of by His Excellency, and with good success. Saddle horses in numbers also awaited the summons of those who would explore by this means, and altogether the members wanted for little on their outing.

According to Else and Rupert, George was very impressed with the airplanes and the fancy lifestyle of the Governor General's entourage. The opportunity to associate with the Governor General and some of the other prominent people for a few days was a special occasion for him. In April 1938, *National Geographic* magazine published an article about Lord Tweedsmuir's trip, and George appeared in one of the photographs.

Shortly afterwards, George was hired by the BC Water Rights Branch. One of their employees left, so George worked for them from August 25 until the end of the field season on September 19.

In Else's February 1938 diary entry, she described events during the end of summer and fall: "Later in September Georg brought some surveyors, Eric Watt among them, who came with us to Hensons so that I saw the place at the [east] end of the lake again for the first time in seven years." With the money George earned, "we bought our first sofa and two comfortable arm chairs. I painted everything and hung new curtains. Both upstairs rooms were freshened up and now both children have their own rooms."

They decided to discontinue the beaver farm because "Georg found some of them dead, it looked like they had mauled each other. We gave the remaining ones to a neighbor who fenced in a small lake, where they can live in more

Camp at Intata Lake. T. W. S. Parsons photograph. Royal BC Museum, BC Archives J-00861

natural conditions. It's not worth raising beavers for fur. It takes 3 years until they are grown and they have only 2–4 young per year."

George had a productive fall trapping season: "He returned with marten, mink, fisher and fox furs that he sold for $200 and bought provisions with the money." Else noted that they were able to celebrate Christmas and the children's birthdays.

For the school's Christmas concert "Rupert was in a play for the first time and Gloria recited her first poem... Santa Claus came with a small sewing machine and presents for the children, and nuts and apples for everyone. Then Rupert's 9th birthday. Hephata and Christmas and games for us with many candles and presents. A New Year's dance with kissing at midnight and going to bed at six in the morning."

Else's next diary entry was almost six months later, near the end of July 1938, and her pessimism had returned.

> It's the middle of summer. Writing is far from my mind. Daily life is the same as always. There was no rain since the snow melted. The grass is yellow and the farmers harvested only small loads of hay and that's all. Parts of the garden are empty and barren. Only on a new small patch, that Georg waters by hauling up water in barrels with the wheelbarrow, grow beans and cabbages and sweet German lupines. That is all. Enough, but yet too little. No income. Georg has been at home now for 4 months and worked only for 9 days at the Tahtsa River. That is very little work. We would not have any clothes to wear if I had not brought clothes for the children and me from Germany. I rack my brains what to do.

Else commented that she was not receiving much mail from Germany. But she took solace in reading: "At night I live in all ages, with the most renowned thinkers and poets as my friends. My bed is surrounded by bookshelves and all I have to do is stretch out my hands to get the minds from all around the world." In contrast to her mood, she noted that "Georg is always busy and optimistic. He wants to go prospecting again and look for gold, like he already did a hundred times." Perhaps the difficult economic conditions prompted her to resume her literary work: "I wrote 'Honeymoon in a Trap Cabin' in English and 'Hephata' in German."

Else's 1938 pocket notebook, which began on April 8, details the family's situation and their interactions with the people around them. On that day, she noted George's return from trapping with a catch of eight marten. Buster

Rupert, Else and Gloria outside their home. University of Victoria Archives 3-32-8

and Cliff Harrison, one of the first people in the area to have a snowmobile, gave him a ride on the last part of his journey.

Almost every day someone stopped for coffee or tea, and Else regularly baked cookies or cake. Occasionally, people stayed for supper. George would sometimes go and help other people. Jimmy Andrews continued to visit the family. On April 14, Else wrote that Andrews had dinner with them, and a couple of times she noted him stopping for coffee. On April 20, she recorded that George and Rupert went to help Bill Walters, while Mrs. Ed Harrison, three of her children, and Bob Nelson came for a five o'clock tea. Eight days later, George helped Ed Harrison at the Harrison sawmill. Beginning on May 5, she recorded the nine days of roadwork that George did. On Sunday, May 8, Bill Walters brought a plough and George spent the day ploughing. There were three guests for dinner, company in the afternoon, and four guests for supper. George spent the following Sunday ploughing again, and Bob Nelson brought seed. Billy Harrison and Jimmy Morgan arrived from Burns Lake with food that Else had ordered.

Hinsche came and stayed for a couple of days. While he was at the Seel house, he sowed the flower garden. Else knew that Hinsche had very little

A photograph of Hinsche taken after he left Ootsa when the property where he lived was flooded. Seel family collection.

food, so she gave him a sack of potatoes and a dozen eggs. Baptiste also visited a few times. On May 17, he came to get a sack of potatoes and drink tea. Events similar to these activities continued throughout 1938.

Else visited neighbours at their homes, and occasionally went with them on outings. One day she went fishing with Beatrice Carroll. She and Gloria joined a group of people on a day trip to Burns Lake. There they did some shopping and on the return trip visited Mrs. Henkel at François Lake. One day George took the whole family, along with Mrs. McNeill and some of her friends, for a picnic at Soda Springs. On Sunday, August 7, the family took a boat trip east along Ootsa Lake. They had lunch with Hinsche, and did some shopping at Schreiber's store. Ernie Harrison came for supper and Baptiste brought moose meat.

Else noted occasions when George worked with Bill McNeill. At the end of June, during July and in early August, he spent several days working on the Tahtsa River. On July 25, Ed van Tine and Ed Mohr took George with them to check a possible forest fire on the north side of the Tahtsa River. They returned the following day and reported no fire.

On August 25, Else wrote: "Canning caribou meat in the morning. Young Indian woman comes to get meat." Else likely got a portion of the caribou in return. Four days later, "Georg goes early with Cap McNeill [Bill's son], Dick Schreiber and a man from the Philippines to Whitesail and Pondosy."

Picnic at Soda Springs. University of Victoria Archives 4-6-41.

[McNeill's Circle Guide business was growing and he occasionally needed additional help.] He returned on September 2 "in afternoon with man from Philippines, guide from Bella Coola, and two boys." A week later, the man from the Philippines and two other men came by car to visit George. The next day the McNeill family, Jack Knox and Skins came by car for a visit. Later the Mohr family came by automobile and stayed until eleven o'clock in the evening.

In mid-October, Else wrote in her diary that the harvest was finished and difficult economic conditions continued.

> The seasons continue: fall is here. Wondrous yellow and gold colours and clear days. Our small harvest is now in the root house. Enough potatoes and turnips to eat. Canned berries and caribou meat that Georg brought back from prospecting. He actually found some ore with a little bit of gold in it... Now he is back out there, continuing his search. No income at all. I sold 2 old gold bracelets, one ring, a few other bits and bobs, to buy shoes for the kids. Both of them go to school every morning.

Else believed that war in Europe was imminent: "Soon there will be war in Europe. Hitler wanted the Sudeten Germans. Mussolini blared out a speech in Trieste that I heard at 2 a.m. at night—an eerie chorus like in a

Greek tragedy: il Duce, Duce... stomping, drilled words; the same with Hitler at the Sportpalast in Berlin: Sieg Heil, Sieg Heil... The masses gone mad, and the people have to live with it."

Around Ootsa Lake, subsistence and persistence continued. Else wrote: "Everyone here muddles along on his or her own account. Now and then people form a co-op and work in a collective. Other than that, everyone takes whatever he can."

J. M. Frank once again planned to visit Wistaria, and Else was disappointed that he did not make the trip. Else also wrote about dreams that reflected her pessimistic outlook: "I often dream of Death who comes to me looking rather old-fashioned, with a scythe and wearing a red cape (as I once saw as a teenager in Kolberg in a school exhibition), and I was smiling while I walked with him along a train track."

But she finished her entry with a more optimistic comment: "During the day I still walk along Ootsa Lake with the children and Beatrice Carroll and her children. We stop for a picnic on a rock bluff. Golden leaves, scattered by the wind, fall into our tea cups and onto the lake. They float for as long as they can—just like us."

On December 1, Else wrote: "Georg was here for 4 days with the first furs, but Norman didn't want to buy them. For the past two weeks I didn't have a cent."

In her pocket notebook, Else recorded that George left on October 1 and returned on November 3 with one fisher and ten mink. Five days later he left in a snowstorm, returning on December 16 with only one marten. They celebrated Rupert's tenth birthday with a big dinner, inviting two of his friends and some neighbours for the occasion. Christmas was a quiet day with only a couple of guests for dinner.

At the back of her 1938 pocket notebook Else kept a record of their income and expenses between May and December. There was no income in May but only four dollars in expenses. In June, George received $41.47 for roadwork and $64.23 for furs. From this income, they paid forty dollars that they owed the store at Schreiber's and they had forty dollars in expenses. For July, George received thirty-nine dollars for his work on the Tahtsa River, and they received a cheque for seventy dollars from Little Brothers for furs. Their expenses were almost equal to their income, with thirty dollars paid to Schreiber's. The only income in August was $4.76 for the two days checking the fire on the Tahtsa River. However, their expenses only amounted to $12.20, with $8.20 going to Eaton's for school clothing for the children. In September, George received twenty dollars for his work with the trip to Whitesail and Pondosy Lake. This equalled their expenses, half of which went to Eaton's for winter clothing. There was no income in October but twenty-five dollars in expenses. George's trap licence cost ten dollars. The family had no income in November, but in December George sold furs for thirty-seven dollars, the same amount as their expenses for those two months.

Else also had a pocket notebook for daily events in 1939. George remained at home during the first six weeks of the year. Much of the time was spent cutting firewood, including three days for the school. George and Else also painted their bedroom. On February 14, George left to go trapping. During the winter there was not as much visiting with the neighbours, but there were occasional activities. On February 24, Else wrote: "Surprise party at our house postponed. Nevertheless, Buster's [family] and Beatrice come, 8 people. We have coffee at midnight!" The next day Rupert left in the morning to go fishing at Eastern Lake, returning in the late afternoon with thirteen trout.

In early March, Else wrote in her diary. "I only went once on skis around the lake. It was fun and I felt young and fresh. How modest! For one week it was 60 below zero, otherwise the winter is quite mild. Chickadees are already chirping and flying around in groups. Yes, spring will be here soon."

Else mentioned that: "The radio stopped working but I am glad. There was a lot of anti-German sentiment because of the persecution of Jews."

She continued writing in an effort to bring some income. On March 24 she commented in her diary: "Today I start writing 'Junges Mädchen wandert aus' [Young Girl Emigrates]. May it be completed and be good. Last night I lay awake and thought about it." Later in the same entry, she declared: "I should get away from here. The circle is complete, but where should I go with two children and without a cent. The only way to run away is by writing, and that's what I am trying to do."

She described two communal activities. "On the 17th, St. Patrick's Day, we had a masquerade for the first time in 11 years. I was dressed up as a Chinese man and won a leather briefcase... Mary Kerr, who is now Mrs. Ford, dressed up in the same 'Monte Carlo' costume that she wore 11 years ago. And one always thinks times are changing." The second event was at their house: "Yesterday a dozen people were here for tea: old Mrs. H. and Beatrice and both Walters, and the Indian woman Baptiste with a newborn baby, tightly strapped into her very old basket that swings on her back like a little gondola."

Else wrote about Rupert's contribution to their food supply: "Every day Rupert catches ling, large and heavy with huge heads. We all live off those fish: the chickens get the head, the guts are for the cat and we eat the meat."

George returned from trapping at the end of March. In her pocket notebook, Else described events that occurred during the Easter weekend in early April. On Good Friday, "Old Chief Louis is here for dinner. Holidays. Here for tea are Mrs. Bill [Harrison], Marion, Mrs. Ed [Harrison], Esther, Irene, Chief Louie." The next day Beatrice Carroll brought a bunch of daffodils and grape hyacinths and stayed for dinner. Else also hid the Easter eggs. On Sunday: "Easter! The children look for Easter eggs. Washing dishes, tidying up. Cooking lunch, Jimmy Andrews and Chief Louie. Pearl, Tootsie, Bill Roberts, Mr. Nellis, the teacher, Frank W[alters] come for tea and stay for supper. Ernie too. They stay until 9 p.m. Nice day."

On April 11, George left to trap again, returning in ten days with two muskrat. Near the end of April, Baptiste and his wife came to their house with their sick baby, and Else gave them some medicine. Much of May was spent working in the garden and constructing a new root cellar. On Sunday, May 14, with the lake now free of ice, the family took a boat trip along Ootsa Lake to visit Hinsche and go to the Schreiber store. After they returned home, Ootsa Lake resident Jimmy Morgan and two children, who were out for a boat trip, stopped for a visit.

In a diary entry in early June, Else commented on the difficult circumstances around Ootsa Lake.

> People here don't have any money... Now the children in the bay don't have any clothes. Georg had only 4 marten all winter and now nothing since Easter. We all live on fish and moose meat and potatoes and rhubarb. Yesterday we were at the Carroll's and laughed about our plight. Beatrice's children ran around in bathing suits. They don't go to school because it's too far away. We fished for trout in Eagle Canyon. I was grateful for a day outside after all those months at the cooking stove and rode across the nameless creek on a tree trunk.

She described her literary efforts.

> I wrote 3 Canadian novels: "Mrs. King and the golden wedding anniversary" and "Hephata." Anita [a German friend who lived in Canada] sent "Hephata" to her sister in Berlin who gave it to an editor who thought it was a good and remarkable piece of work. That's everything I heard so far. J. M. Frank sent me a book "I lived wrongly." I cannot read it. I cannot even translate the title for the people here. They just don't understand how one can "live wrongly" and I don't believe it either. Life is a logical sequence of building and growing. We grow like trees or we violate the natural laws and wither. Only in Berlin one can "live wrongly."

The main audience for Else's literary work was in Germany, but the opportunity to reach that audience was diminishing as the threat of war increased.

People at Wistaria tried to maintain their community spirit despite their difficult situation. Several of them gathered for a picnic, games and dancing at the schoolhouse on a Sunday in late June. They also held their annual Dominion Day picnic.

George had no work during the summer, so there was no income for the family. Rupert spent much of his time fishing, bringing in additional food for the family. After finishing all of the work that needed to be done around the house, George left to go prospecting on July 15.

In mid-July Else wrote: "Georg is away prospecting for the past three days, deep in the mountains where he hasn't been before and where there is gold according to the Indians. He probably believes in it, childish as always. I don't and hope that I am wrong."

While George was away, Else maintained the household. Rupert helped with chores and continued fishing. In her pocket notebook, Else described George's return on August 19: "Georg comes home at noon, limping. He didn't catch anything, had a sore leg and rheumatism. Very disappointed."

On September 1, Germany invaded Poland. Two days later, Great Britain and France declared war on Germany, the beginning of World War II in Europe. Canada joined the Allies on September 10. On September 14, Else wrote about this momentous event and her reaction to events. Since the radio wasn't working and she hadn't read anything yet, her knowledge of the situation was limited.

> I heard that there is war. I haven't heard or seen anything. But there is war in Germany, with Germany. Germany against Poland, England and France. The Germans are in Warsaw and the French in Saarbrücken. The radio doesn't work and the magazines and weekly newspapers haven't published anything yet. Should I experience this war from so far away while I was right in the middle of the first one? No, that's not possible. I don't want to be safe and far away. I want to taste and feel things again even if they are bitter, very bitter. I had enough of the loneliness and the broken shoes. We didn't make a cent for the past six months. Georg came back, skin and bones. He had rheumatism again, hat fallen off somewhere and the only reason he told me because he wanted me to pity him. But I don't have any compassion any more, not even for myself. The summer was no summer. A few flowers blossomed in front of

> the window and froze soon after and looked ugly. I don't go outside. Where should I go? To hear how all the people hate Hitler and Germany? At least when they come into the house they hold back. The children are happy and healthy and don't notice anything. They play noisily and go to school and learn something. Rupert shot his first willow grouse with a slingshot and contributes some food. Food is scarce: potatoes and berries that I had canned, and sometimes cabbage. Everything else froze or got eaten by the worms.
>
> No more letters are coming from Germany. The last link breaks. Georg didn't say good-bye when he left ten days ago; this link is broken too. What is left? Only a weak and squeamish little soul that at one time wanted to do so much and conquer the world. But that requires a different type. War! What for? Why? Danzig, Poland, England? The Empire sinks.

Else ended her entry with a literary reference to the unsettling circumstances: "Little apple, where are you rolling?"

Fortunately for the Seel family, George got work with Bill McNeill clearing the Tahtsa River in October and November. He left on October 4 and returned October 23. George left again on November 7 and returned on December 14. It appears that he worked on the Tahtsa River for a few weeks and then did some trapping. The income from the river work was especially important since George's trapping did not yield any furs.

In mid-February, Else wrote about the 1939 holiday season.

> Christmas was dismal. Almost no presents except for what I had made or sewed myself and a few compassionate souls sent parcels for the children who were so happy with the small things they got. Georg came back from trapping without a single pelt since there had been snow, rain, and then more snow. It is terrible, he cannot make an income from the wilderness with his bare hands. Everything is in vain. And I sit here as the months go by, getting duller and quieter. Rupert turned 11. He is growing up, becomes more understanding, catches squirrels and weasels and made his first money that he used to buy some pants. He goes fishing and brings us trout.

Although Christmas was quiet and a sombre time, there was a celebration that Else recorded in her pocket notebook on December 27: "At 9 p.m. 22 people came for a surprise party. Games and dancing until 2 a.m."

Else again kept a record of their income and expenses in 1939. In January, the ten mink George trapped the previous fall brought seventy-one dollars. All of that money went to Schreiber's store, and in addition they had eleven dollars in expenses. The next month the fisher and marten brought fifty-two dollars, of which thirty-five dollars were paid to the Schreibers, along with thirteen dollars in expenses. The weasel and squirrels that Rupert trapped yielded five dollars in March, the only income for the month. Fortunately, they only had six dollars in expenses. In May, fifty-three dollars were earned in trapping income, with almost all of the money going to Schreiber's store. During the next four months there was only five dollars of income, but expenses were less than twenty dollars. George received a hundred and ten dollars in both October and November for work on the Tahtsa River. This provided vital income for the family. Fifty dollars in the first month went to paying off their debt with Schreiber's, and a hundred dollars was spent in November buying a large quantity of food from the local store. There was no income in December.

The 1930s began in a time of economic uncertainty and was a decade of hardship for most people around the world. It ended with a potentially more devastating uncertainty, another world war. The war caused particular concern for George and Else. They were Canadian citizens, but they had been born in Germany, and they did not know how the Canadian government would treat them, especially since there were internment camps in the country in World War I. Else was worried about her mother and brother and had no easy way to communicate with them. An even greater concern was how the children would be treated, for they had been born and raised in Canada. Else and George also did not know if the start of the war would affect their relationships with the people of the Ootsa Lake area, especially their neighbours around Wistaria.

Rejuvenation

The new decade did not have a good beginning for Else and George. In mid-February Else received a letter informing her that her mother had died on January 2. The war had cut communication between Germany and Canada, so the letter had been sent through a friend in New York, for the United States was not yet involved in World War II.

At Wistaria, Else and George maintained normal relationships with most of their neighbours. However, "Old Bill still said loudly: all Germans should be eliminated (kill them, wherever they are)." It must have been difficult for

Gloria, Else and George in a new boat that George built in 1940. University of Victoria Archives 4-6-47

Else to hear these words, for Old Bill had been a friend since she first arrived at Wistaria, and he had always been kind to her. Else also found church difficult: "I go to church but cannot pray since the reverend asks God for his blessings for the British army."

On June 1 Else expressed her discomforting thoughts: "Spring is gone and summer is here... In Europe there is war. One country after another falls into its grip... I have stomach pains for I am sick of the world. Perhaps I have cancer. Then I would wish for a quick ending."

She also wrote: "We ploughed, sowed and planted, the only thing we could do. We will continue to work if no higher power tears us away. If only the children learn to respect the important things in life. It is my greatest wish that they will grow above the dollar and not into it. For myself I don't wish anything anymore. My mother is dead, my home country is dead, and my life has become small. 'Whatever exists is worth perishing' says Goethe. What could I add to this?"

The school at Wistaria in 1940. Rupert is in the front row to the right (facing the camera) of the girl wearing the white dress, while Gloria is in the front with the patterned dress. Else Seel photograph. University of Victoria Archives 4-6-47

After the trapping season finished, George did not have any work for several months and the family faced difficult financial conditions once again.

When she next wrote on September 24, she commented on how peaceful life was at Ootsa Lake. She was glad that the children were safe and living there, compared to the bombings in Europe and people hiding underground.

George finally got some employment, work from Bill McNeill.

> Georg is prospecting for the last time. Before that he went on the Circle trip with 2 old ladies from New York, 60 and 70 years old, but very fit. Mrs. Vincent painted Georg in front of his tent, with his pipe, and the mountains in the background. It was the first income in 6 months and we paid the store bill that is always lurking in the background.
>
> Gloria and I were out only once, at the soda springs with Mrs. Brown, the Carroll's and Sievert Anderson from Decker Lake.

They met Hans Klaverwyden, a Dutchman, and his wife, Jeanette. Else noted that "Georg is going to build a basement for them. Then he wants to go to Prince Rupert because there is more work in construction." [Klaverwyden

The McNeills' property at Ootsa Lake. Else Seel photograph. University of Victoria Archives 3-33-50

worked for Shell Oil in China for twenty years prior to coming to Canada in the summer of 1939. He and his wife built a tourist lodge along Ootsa Lake west of Wistaria. Else commented: "Sometimes on their way to the post office they stop by and I like to talk to them."]

In mid-January 1941, Else wrote: "There is a new year again. The years run through my hands like water. For almost 2 months Georg built a basement and a fireplace for Hans, the Dutchman. With the $200 we could pay all our debts and could buy some food and clothes." The fireplace was constructed with stones gathered along the shore of Ootsa Lake. Else took a trip near the end of the year: "At the beginning of December I went to Prince Rupert for a week to go to the dentist. I was happy to get out for a week for the first time in three years and enjoyed every minute of it."

When World War II started, the Allied countries lost access to some important materiel. This included mercury, which was used for bomb detonators. In the 1930s, the major source of mercury had been from mines in Spain. There had been a civil war in Spain between 1936 and 1939 and, although Spain was officially neutral during World War II, its leader, Francisco Franco, was sympathetic to the Axis countries of Germany and Italy, making Spain's large supply of mercury unavailable to the Allies. Another country that produced a significant amount of mercury was Italy, but its supply went to the Axis countries. The United States had some mercury mines but it was also officially neutral at the beginning of the war. Russia's main sources of mercury were captured by Germany in 1942.

Wood for the winter. Else Seel photograph. University of Victoria Archives 4-6-47

In 1939, Canada's production of mercury totalled six flasks (35 kilograms per flask). But in 1937, J. G. Gray of the Dominion Geological Survey discovered cinnabar, a rock formation that contained mercury, on the slopes above the north shore of Pinchi Lake northwest of Fort St. James. The area was staked with mineral claims the following year and these were optioned to Consolidated Mining (Cominco), the largest mining company in western Canada. In 1939, Consolidated Mining started operation of the Pinchi mercury mine, with production beginning in 1940. At its peak in 1943, the mine employed over 250 people and produced 22,000 flasks of mercury. It was the largest mercury mine in Canada during the war and for a while was the largest in North America. Not only was the cinnabar mined at Pinchi, the ore was crushed and roasted in kilns there, producing the mercury on site.

The mine provided employment to many people in the Central Interior of British Columbia and helped spark an economic recovery in the region. A few men from Wistaria, including Ed Harrison, obtained employment there. George went to Pinchi in late April 1941 where he found that there were a lot of people looking for work. However, the mine did not have anyone with masonry skills. He wrote to Else from Fort St. James: "I was at Pinchi yesterday & had a long talk with the manager especially about his revolving kilns having endless trouble. There are two & anytime one falls down it means half shift with great loss." George inspected one and found that improper mortar joints were the cause, but he had to wait until the construction engineer returned the next day before he could be hired. George wrote that "He put me in the book as stone mason & should get wages accordingly." George also noted that he would probably get overtime After seeing all the people working or looking for work at Pinchi, George told Else: "I realize now that Rupert must learn a good trade."

In August, Else wrote in her diary: "Georg went to Pinchi Lake on May 1 to work as a mason in a mercury mine. He makes $150 per month but food, lodging, and smaller expenses amount to $50. The first $100 that he made were paid to the store, and the second $100 for much needed shoes, socks, things for the children and for Georg, and a new double bed."

George wrote Else a letter in mid-May: "I am working with Bill Harrison most of the time putting up frames & casing for concrete walls & everything is going smoothly. No one bothers us." He noted that he was being paid carpenter's wages, but once he began lining the furnace and retorts he would receive additional pay. George also commented that "they have not taken anybody since I came here." In June, George told Else that there were now two masons working at the mine, along with sixty carpenters and the general labourers. He described the "2 million fire bricks here now for the 7 story kilns & machinery, the likes I have never seen before, the whole place filled up & still coming, about 200 men working here now." He commented: "Writing 3 letters is real work for me with all the noise outside."

George came home in July for a vacation, and Else and Rupert accompanied him on a short prospecting trip to the Eutsuk Lake area. Else described this adventure in detail in her diary.

> I woke up early in the morning at 3 a.m. It was windy and still dark. I woke Georg and Rupert and half an hour later we had our things loaded onto the boat and were ready to go. Windy point was windy indeed. It got greyer and lighter. A young moose swam straight towards us from the shore and we scared it back with the boat. As soon as we entered the mouth of the river the water became calm. The sun rose, casting beautiful colours, purple and blue, on the water and on the mountains. Ducks were splashing around and seagulls who were not afraid of us were sitting quietly on the water. At 7 a.m. we had breakfast at Pole Camp: eggs and bacon and thousands of mosquitoes. We hurried to move on, 16 miles [25 kms] along Long [Sinclair] Lake and then along the fast Whitesail Lake River that was so shallow that Georg had to get into the water to pull the boat, while Rupert pushed with a long pole. He wanted to fish and we stopped near an eddy. Rupert caught a big fish and we stopped, lit a fire and had the fish for dinner. Then we continued along Whitesail Lake... At the left side of the lake we turned and reached the portage. Magnificent mountains with white peaks were all around, Alpine peaks, Swiss Pilatus, Uri-Rotstock: remember, Else, remember... (42 miles [67 kms] on the first day).
>
> We spent the first night under tall trees in the pristine forest, with the stars directly above our sleeping faces. The campfire glowed. There was a splash in the water, owls, and a few curious squirrels that came very close. Then morning came and birds were calling. We got up early and loaded everything on the tram cart that Georg had to get from the other side. A miniature rail track through the pristine forest—half a mile long. We had to go uphill and pushed hard. Going downhill, I sat at the front end and pulled up my legs carefully so that they didn't get caught in the bushes on the side. We went through a bog with tall wild grass, mullein, blue lupines, six-foot fireweed,

swarms of insects whirling around, an intoxicating scent, then came again tall pines and fir trees, poplars and undergrowth. All of a sudden the track went downhill towards blue water and a bay; Big Eutsuk. We found a boat named "Pondosy" and put our things in there, attached the motor and went on. Around bays and canyons, around Iron point, where the water formed a whirlpool and the small boat bounced around crazily. The mountains got closer and closer and evening came, and we stopped at Bill Grell's Cove. Bill Grell... painted simple pictures like the ones you would see on wayside crosses, and he had built a trapping cabin here. Rupert slept there and we slept in Frank Knowles cabin, high up on a small hill, well-furnished and even equipped with a radio. Trapping has become modern...

We had our morning coffee and continued for another 12 miles [20 kilometres] on the Big Eutsuk. There were Big Bear and Little Bear Island and then came the short and swift Pondosy River with protruding pointed rocks. It bubbled and rushed and then it was quiet again. Grey-green water, steep mountains with glaciers right by the lake, and Pondosy Lake, our destination. Hundreds of seagulls were flying in the air. It was much cooler. We could see a small cabin and went towards it. The boat grated along the light coloured gravel. We built a fire place, hung two cooking pots above it, fried a bannock in the open frying pan and had a great meal.

The next morning Georg went prospecting on the mountain for two days and Rupert and I stayed by ourselves. Rupert went fishing but didn't catch anything, so he built a shipyard out of poplars and I lay in the sun until it disappeared and it started to rain. In the cabin I found some Wild West and detective stories and I flipped through the pages. The same stuff that I read sitting in the attic at Schivelbein when I was 12 years old. The mentality of those trappers is no different. They brought radios all the way to these corners of the world and listen to Jack Benny and Amos and Andy—I would like to know how this is supposed to be romantic.

On the evening of the second day Georg came back and I greeted him with a steaming mulligan, cooking in the pot on the fire. We ate and talked and he showed me samples that he could not identify. What an unsure thing this whole enterprise is!

George (left) and Rupert at the portage between Whitesail Lake and Eutsuk Lake. Else Seel photograph. University of Victoria Archives 9-6-1

His knowledge of ores is insufficient; all he knows is from hearsay. And I have waited faithfully for 15 years! Oh you sheep—where is the romanticism? There is nothing but wearing old clothes and frayed shoes and a diet of fish and game meat. But it doesn't upset me—I know now the limitation of the world and its pleasures.

Early in the morning we headed home. Pondosy Lake was wavy as we left. The seagulls flew all around us, on this real, small inland ocean with grey-green, ice cold water and snowy mountains. The short Pondosy River was fast and wild, and there were sharp rocks in the water. Again we passed the Small Bear and Big Bear and stopped in Beaver Creek to get gasoline. It got windier as we crossed Big Eutsuk to get to Bill Grell's cove to cook. On the hill with the small trapping cabin I lay in the sun for a while, while Georg and Rupert followed a fresh bear track. Once they were back I got impatient and wanted to move on. We packed up and travelled two miles [3.2 kilometres] but then began the dangerous part of the great lake: Iron Point, where the wind howled from all directions, creating eddies and waves. We had to wait and lay around the fire under a tall cedar. It smelled wonderful, and I sang with the village children: Under your arborvitae we will be dreaming... and my father's copper coffin was being carried past us to the train station. Wasn't that the reason that I was here in the Canadian wilderness? The sun went down but it didn't get dark—the northern night. And I jumped into the boat and said, "Let's go!" and I almost wished that the whirlpools would swallow me up. However, we did make it through the 6 miles [10 kilometres] of watery hell. It rushed and hissed all around us and the small boat almost turned itself around. Rupert made a small, scared face that I hadn't seen before. We all held on. A big ragged rock stared at us threateningly… The clouds dashed along above us and the waves splashed unto my clothes and in my face. Yes, a bit of romanticism is still here, at midnight at Iron Point in the Big Eutsuk… Dead tired, we finally slept under tall trees at Surveyor's Point.

We woke up before sunrise. Now the water was calm and we were gliding along, almost like in a dream. There stood a moose at the shore, browsing in the water lilies. It lifted its head and looked quietly at us, without moving, even though the engine made a lot of noise. Even when Georg turned off the engine and took his carbine the moose remained still; a perfect target. I felt so sorry for it, but we needed the meat. Georg shot and the bullet hit. The moose was still standing in the same spot and just slumped down a bit. Another shot, and another one. Very slowly the animal went into the bushes to die there. When we arrived it was already dead. With a lot of effort I lifted its big head. The mighty antlers were not yet mature, and like velvet. The leaves were red with blood. I moaned, but Georg had already started to cut it up. We carried the haunches, the liver and the heart to the boat.

This time the portage was easier since we had to go downhill. At the end lay our boat like a little dog on a chain. We loaded it up. I fried up the fresh liver with potatoes. We were hungry and had a wonderful meal. The Whitesail was smooth and the sun was blazing hot. Rupert was trolling, but all the fish must have been asleep at the bottom, keeping cool, since they were not taking the bait. We went along the water for hours. The mountains disappeared in the distance and the shore came closer again. On the river we met McNeill with 2 tourists from California. Those people spend hundreds of dollars to go on the same trips that we make. However, they sit in the boat and are scared, with big sunglasses and big sun hats. I greeted them and McNeill said that I looked like a squaw. I took it as a compliment. I was dark brown indeed! Then the evening came and we were on our Ootsa Lake which was tame as a lamb. We crossed it and went ashore at Carroll's. There was Mrs. Allen from Chicago with her two boys and we took them all in our boat to Mrs. Brown. I saw Gloria again—she,

> too was brown and fresh, and Mrs. Allen drove us home in an elegant car.
>
> The next few days were a whirlwind. The meat had to be canned and the fat rendered. We had to pick and can strawberries. The jars in the root house now stand in rows like a small army of soldiers. First 100, then 120 and now 150 jars. Food for the winter. What would the poor people in Europe give for those berries, fish, meat and vegetables. I am now probably richer than they and can feed my children—they don't have to stay hungry. During all those hard years we have become rather modest.

George returned to Pinchi with Alf Harrison in his car. Gloria and Else accompanied the two men. The weather was hot and the roads dusty, so they stopped at the hotel in Endako where the men had a beer and the women ice cream. Else noted that there was a big sawmill at Fraser Lake, and described the area: "Everywhere are forest and small farms and Indian settlements and wooden huts and churches with open bell towers. Also a big Indian school with a garden and fields and a barn where the Indians learn everything from Catholic priests and nuns" (the residential school at Lejac). They stopped at Vanderhoof for a meal: "We eat at a Chinese restaurant and have a look around the small dusty city. Teenage girls and guys sit in front of the drugstore, eating ice cream and drinking orangeade."

After saying good bye to George at Pinchi, Alf, Else and Gloria drove back to Fort St. James and stayed overnight at a hotel. The next day, they returned to Wistaria.

In a diary entry Else made in early January 1942, she noted that Canada was now at war with Japan, and that there were blackouts in Vancouver and Prince Rupert. As well, she wrote that "Georg came back on October 1, made repairs on the house and put a new roof on the house. In November/December he went trapping and brought back 5 marten and some small stuff. We couldn't sell anything because the prices were low due to the war, but then went up again and we made $90 on the best marten at Little Bros. in Vancouver."

George returned to work at Pinchi early in 1942.

Else wrote notes in English chronicling some of the events that occurred during 1942: "Slowly the numbers of men around here are dwindling. All young people, including some girls join the military. All other men up to 60 years of age are soaked up by the industry. Only women and children stay behind."

She commented that Mrs. Ed Harrison often came to visit while her husband was working at Pinchi. Her eldest son was in the army and one of her daughters went to Fort St. James, leaving Mrs. Harrison at home with her three youngest children.

Else described the situation at Wistaria.

> Sometimes one of the women harnesses the horses and we take the sleigh to another family in the settlement. We sit around the oven and talk about our everyday life. I get wood and water, feed the chickens and cows and bake and cook. It seems to be a second self that does all that, only half aware of what it is doing while it is listening to the world where the war rages wild and wilder. Now and then I get news of someone's death through the Red Cross: my brother, the only son of my friend, Rainer. How bitter did he speak in 1937 at the age of 16 of the military education, read Tolstoy, and died in combat at Stalingrad.

Tragedy struck in July when Mrs. Ed Harrison "drowned herself last night. The women came running and wanted to know if she was with me." The funeral was held at the Harrison home: "When the coffin was carried out of the house nobody wanted to follow, so I went first. After all she had been my nearest neighbour for 15 years and we had tea together hundreds of times." In several of her diary entries over the years, Else had written about Mrs. Harrison being listless and depressed. The stress of wartime conditions had probably exacerbated the situation for her. Else wrote a poem expressing her thoughts about her neighbour and friend.

Mrs. Ed's death appeared to affect George, who came home unexpectedly: "He wants to take me and the kids with him to Fort St. James this winter. We will rent a cabin at the hotel and live there. We packed, locked everything up and left the animals with the neighbours." While George was home, he went prospecting in the Tahtsa River area and staked a claim on Placer Creek. This was the same area where he thought that he had found gold in 1932. The area had heavy forest cover and only a few outcrops, so the claim was never developed.

George returned to work at Pinchi, and Else and the children came on Labour Day weekend. They rented a small cabin along the lake that was owned by Mrs. Jones (formerly Mrs. Forfar), proprietress of the nearby hotel. The children liked the larger school and quickly made friends. Sometimes Rupert went to the float plane base and helped the famous bush pilot Russ Baker load and unload his plane. George worked at Pinchi but came to Fort St. James almost every weekend. Else made new friends, including Mrs. Wahl, who had been a teacher in Vienna and ran a dairy business; the German hotel manager; and Miss Adams, Rupert's teacher, who had a great interest in books and literature.

The Neighbour
Else Seel, translated by Claudia Golombiewski

I saw you coming across the hill,
I saw your dress fluttering:
Ootsa blew into your wings,
You flew way too far.

Alas, the hands are so narrow
and face and hair are so thin,
You came from London's poor parts,
and life was too hard.

Alas, the winter was so long,
and it made your face pale,
and it bleached your hair,
but it did not give you any strength.

Casually you lowered your hands,
casually you left house and garden;
I saw you waving a hundred times
and saw you wear away more and more.

I wanted to encourage you, and
wanted to do good things for you,
but after all those bouts of life
all you wanted to do was rest, yes, rest.

And during a summer's night
you went quietly down to the lake;
Your children were sleeping peacefully,
nobody was near you.

DIE NACHBARIN
Else Seel

Sah Dich kommen ueberm Huegel,
sah Dein Flatternd Kleid:
Ootsa blies in Deine Fluegel,
flogest viel zu weit.

Ach, so schmal die Haende
und so duenn Gesicht und Haar,
kamst aus London's armen Ende,
und das Leben war zu bar.

Ach, so lang der Winter war,
und er bleichte Dein Gesicht,
und er bleichte auch Dein Haar,
nur die Kraefte gab er nicht.

Laessig liesst Du Deine Haende sinken,
laessig liesst Du Haus und Garten stehn;
hundertmal sah ich Dich winken
und Dich mehr und mehr vergehn.

Wollte Dir noch Mut einfloessen,
wollte Dir noch Gutes tun
doch nach all den Lebensstoessen
wolltest Du nur ruhn, ja, ruhn.

Und in einer Sommernacht
gingst Du schweigend in den See;
Deine Kinder schliefen sacht,
niemand war in Deiner Naeh.

Else resumed writing a diary when she was at Fort St. James but began to write in English and started using the English spelling of George. In early October, she and the children spent a Sunday walking around Fort St. James. She wrote: "Home around 7, we find a bag of apples and the *Sonnets from the Portuguese* by Elizabeth Barrett Browning right at our doorstep. From Miss Adams, Rupert's superior teacher, and I went to bed very happy with the decadent sonnets from another century."

Hallowe'en was on Saturday and Else described the events of the weekend: "Halloween was a big day. The children had a party at school and Gloria went as a witch. George came home in the afternoon, and getting dark, the whole school went off with black smeared faces or masks before them to beg apples and candy from every house. They came back loaded with oranges, apples, candy, cookies and even money. On our door knocked a whole gang too, and some Indian boys and girls." The adults had a dance in the community hall that started at midnight. When Else and George went home at 4:00 am, the dance was still continuing. Else wrote that, "We spent the Sunday together—a happy little family: George and Rupert cutting wood along the beach, Gloria and I cooking and washing the dishes. For the evening we went to Reichhold's. He played the piano really good, with a self-composed waltz; then all the German melodies. He looked at me if I remembered—I remembered all right, only the words were not more there—gone with the wind in 15 years."

On November 9, Else wrote: "My birthday! During the night I got up and looked out the window. The boys were still on the frozen Stuart Lake skating around burning wood fires... I had a pang in my heart, growing older and older and nothing done for mankind. It sure is not enough to raise a little family. What else can I do for mankind? This morning I found a saucer with candy from Rupert on the table and a box of chocolates from Gloria—the first birthday presents from the children."

Else described a dramatic event that occurred in the late fall.

> The nice big hotel burned down in the night of the 7th of December. We were all asleep: Rupert and Gloria in the kitchen and I in the bedroom. Around 1 o'clock I awoke from some shouting: "Get out, come on, quick, etc"... I jumped out of bed and ran to the kitchen to look out the window. The big lobby windows of the hotel were scarlet. I shouted to the children, "Get up, quick, the hotel is on fire. Dress yourself, all your warm things, coat and caps too." Then I jumped in my clothes, fine coat and hand bag and grabbed some blankets. I ran out and spread them on

> the snow so far as I could go to the fence corner and told the children to pack out what they could.
>
> The hotel was a big mass of flames. The guests had to jump from the second floor, one man burned to death. I went back again for our clothing, nothing insured, so if it burned, we would have nothing... The cabin was lighted by tremendous flames and hot like a stove... If the snow had not protected the roof this little wood building would have gone in no time. The people must have thought the same. Two soldiers came over to help us save the things. They took the smaller cupboard, but half outside the doors opened and my jars and the dishes came out with a rush. So they left it right there and blocked the doorway...
>
> The hotel was one big flame right up to the sky. So I came out [of] the house with another armful of blankets, and of all things a 3 lb. box of coffee which I had saved for Christmas.

A man saw her, grabbed her by the arm, dragged her to the street and told her to stay there beside Mrs. Jones, the hotel owner. Later:

A photograph of the Pinchi mine at the time that George worked there. Royal BC Museum, BC Archives J-08667

> Miss Adams took my arm and we went to the hotel and looked at the fire. The greatest might of the flames was gone, the wall of the house with the empty windows collapsed inside. The terrible heat had the snow and ice all around melted away—it was a pool of water, a mirror for the flames. People standing around, trying to look for the body of the man... Miss Adams helped us packing the things in again. It was around 4 o'clock in the morning... Rupert and Gloria had made their beds again and were already asleep. I stayed up all night, once in a while watching the fire which flared up again, but its force was broken. The nice hotel where I had spent a beautiful night with George, the lobby with the big windows, the moose horns and mounted fish and all the fine photos were gone forever.

At the end of January 1943, Else described events that occurred during the past two months. For Rupert's fourteenth birthday his friend from Wistaria, Ernie Harrison, came from Kamloops. He and a classmate of Rupert's joined the family for dinner. For Christmas they had a "big table with presents: clothing, slippers, blanket, books, games and something to eat—more than thousands of people have in Europe. How often I think of them and everything is overshadowed." Else got a book from a friend and two books from Miss Adams. They celebrated New Year's at the Wahl home where there were twelve people and a table loaded with food.

In January they had two weeks of cold weather with the temperature around −40°C.

> The children had no school, just sitting around the stove reading *Life* and *Newsweek* and *Saturday Evening Post*, listening to the radio a little. The war goes on and on; the reporters killing every German soldier, but still there seem to be some alive yet. George home for a night and half a day: a tooth knocked out by the crusher. So he pays for the war too. Rationing: ½ lb. [225 grams] butter a week. I have to smile. Did they ever have ½ lb. a month? This is still the land of plenty yet. I remember the taste of horse meat, not so bad with lots of onion. But the smell of turnips in every house, turnips and potatoes and nothing else! But still we came though, and it is hard to die of starvation here as there are fish in the lake and grouse running right around the cabin so dainty, and lots of deer and moose in the woods.

Else wrote a note about the spring: "We spend a lot of time outside. Mrs. Wahl shows me her new farm and talks about the new house she wants to build. As we walk along we sing our old German songs and melodies from operettas, and she talks about Vienna and I about Berlin."

After her diary entry in January, Else made one final entry on December 8, 1943.

> This year is finished pretty soon. I did not write at all. We stayed in Fort St. James until the end of school and the end of June. George sprained his knee and got his old pains back again. He was very sick for 4 months, 2 weeks in Burns Lake Hospital and a whole month in Pinchi Lake Hospital, just built up like a little glass house. Between here on the couch and very grouchy, and that was the year for me.
>
> I am glad we have this house over our heads. Where should we have gone? So we painted everything over, put wallpaper in the living room, and it is nice and shiny now.
>
> Next week George will be back from Pinchi where he started work again on the 20th of October and we celebrate Christmas with a turkey and building a chimney from bricks.
>
> Rupert is getting 15 years old on December 22nd. A big boy and very willing to work. He earned 100 dollars this summer haying and working on the road.

Else wrote that there was a shortage of teachers, so there was no school at Wistaria that year. Gloria and Rupert were taking correspondence classes and Else was helping them.

She also talked about the war: "We have a warm room and a cow to milk and something to eat. I am grateful. What would we do in Germany? Berlin is bombed every day—all the places I know will be dust and ashes."

George worked at Pinchi until the mine closed in 1944 due to falling prices for mercury. On May 23, George wrote Else from Pinchi: "I just got back from the office, there is a man from Trail named Campbell who is supervising the transfer of men to Trail & Kimberley & he could not send me there on account of being born in Germany. I am the 5th one & he was very sorry—also told me to stick around here & something may turn up... The camp is very much depressed, especially the ones with houses in hand which are a dead loss to them."

While he was at Pinchi, George began planning for changes in the family's life at Wistaria when he returned. He wanted to spend more time at home and do more farming. On April 24, 1944, BC Minister of Lands Wells Gray, reported to Cabinet:

> That an application has been received from George V. Seel of Pinchi Lake, B.C., to lease for hay and grazing purposes the E. 1/2 of Lot 1177, Range 4, Coast District, containing 205 acres [83 hectares], situated in the vicinity of Ootsa Lake;
>
> That the land applied for lies within the boundaries of the reserve established under authority of Order-in-Council No. 1653, approved December 9, 1943, notice of which was published in the British Columbia Gazette of December 16th 1943;
>
> That a report has been received showing the area under application as suitable for the purpose required.

Gray recommended that this parcel of land be removed from the forestry reserve, and on May 1, Cabinet approved the lease of this land to George.

In fall 1944, Rupert accompanied his father on the trapline. They stayed almost until Christmas. On the return trip, Rupert fell through the ice near the shore along Ootsa Lake. George built a fire to warm Rupert, but he was still wet, so they continued walking through the night until they reached the house. When they arrived, they found that it was two days after Christmas. Else, who had been worried, was not pleased at their late arrival.

By 1945, World War II was coming to a close. The post-war era would bring considerable change to the lives of many people, including the Seel family and other residents of Wistaria. For George, much of his work became income-based and it particularly centred on employment in prospecting and logging. On several occasions, George earned more income in a month than he had in an entire year during the Great Depression. After the year at Fort St. James, Rupert did not go to school, although he took courses by correspondence and completed grade 11 and some of his grade 12 program. In 1945, he started working on a regular basis, and the money he earned considerably improved the family's finances. As the children grew up, the family relationships changed too.

In summer 1945, Consolidated Mining hired George on contract to prospect in the Whitesail and Tahtsa area at his discretion, and he was able to employ Rupert as his assistant. This was the first time that Rupert was employed with his father. During the next few years, Rupert worked with George on some projects, learning the skills he needed to work outdoors in rugged conditions, and developing an ethic of hard work and persistence in accomplishing a task.

The 1945 British Columbia Department of Mines annual report described the renewed interest in prospecting in the area of Tahtsa, Whitesail and Eutsuk lakes. It observed: "The area has received attention from prospectors at

A view of the housing at the Pinchi mine site. Royal BC Museum, BC Archives J-08666

various times in the past. Sibola Mountain was, in 1914, the scene of a small stampede occasioned by the discovery of a number of small quartz veins." During the Depression, after Consolidated Mining ceased work on the Emerald Glacier property in 1931, "there was very little prospecting in the country until 1944, when interest was renewed by the discovery of gold-bearing quartz veins on the Harrison group at the west end of Whitesail Lake." The report noted that in 1945 Consolidated Mining "had three two-man prospecting parties in various parts of the area."

George and Rupert spent the summer prospecting in the area near George's trapline south of the Tahtsa River. They backpacked all their supplies for the summer from Tahtsa River along the trail to Troitsa Lake. There was rationing of certain foods during the war, but George and Rupert were allowed extra rations because of the work they were doing for Cominco. At Troitsa Lake, they constructed a raft, and they also found an old dugout canoe that probably belonged to Baptiste Louie. They used both to ferry their supplies up to the head of Troitsa Lake. Along the way, they became wind-bound at a place near the future site of Kingfisher Lodge, and there Rupert carved his name on a tree. They proceeded up the drainage through the Blanket Lakes to Seel Lake, where they prospected along the east side of the Coast Mountains for the summer. Their work did not result in any new mining claims. George and Rupert didn't hear that World War II had ended until they returned in September.

In addition to his work with Cominco, George did some prospecting with friends on the north side of the Tahtsa River. The Department of Mines report described what they located:

> The Riverside group consists of four claims, located by J. W. [Bill] McNeill, J. [Jack] Knox, and George Seel, of Ootsa Landing. The claims are on the north side of Tahtsa River and are reached from a camping ground that is about 1 ½ miles [2.4 kilometres] downstream from the junction of Kasalka (Blue) Creek.
>
> The showing is a new discovery made on the east face of a rocky knoll, about 200 feet [60 metres] above the level of Tahtsa River and about 500 feet [150 metres] from the river's edge.
>
> The main showing consists of mineralization along a fracture striking north 85 degrees east and dipping 80 degrees south... The mineralization extends across a width of from 2 to 5 inches [5 to 12.5 centimetres] and in one place reaches a maximum width of 14 inches [35 centimetres]. The owners report their highest sample assayed 0.36 oz. [10.2 grams] of gold per ton. A picked sample containing 25 per cent arsenopyrite assayed: gold 0.13 oz. [3.7 grams] per ton; silver 0.2 oz. [5.7 grams] per ton.
>
> The Freeport Exploration Company, under the direction of Lamont West, did some surface work on the showing. By means of open cuts the mineralized fracture was traced for about 100 feet [30 metres]. It was uncovered again across a draw about 250 feet [75 metres] to the east.

The report noted that another prospecting group staked four claims adjoining Riverside on the west. The Riverside group, which was less than a kilometre from George's trapping cabin on the Tahtsa River, was a rich showing, but it was very small and was never developed.

The Department of Mines report also described a renewed interest in the area on Swing Peak that George had staked several years previously: "The Captain group consists of six located claims on the northeastern slopes of Swing Peak, covering showings previously held by George Seel and then known as the Swannell group."

With the end of the war, Else "received the first news from Germany: bad news, news of people's deaths, and long lists of the people who died. I was in shock. And everyone was now asking for help... I packed many parcels, put in orders at the store, made butter and packed it in tin cans that I sealed by soldering, ordered Care packages and packages from New York. I spent all the little money I had on those packages and the postage. I did what I could and still it seemed so little for so many people."

During the year, George built a new porch and extension to their home. He purchased two cows with calves. This was the beginning of a small cattle operation, using the land obtained by lease from the provincial government.

George and Rupert spent the first part of the winter of 1945–46 on the trapline. In March, D. C. Malcolm of Cominco's Mines Department wrote to George: "We'll be prospecting in the Whitesail area again this year. Will you let me know if you can go out again and if Rupert will go with you?" George and Rupert spent much of the summer of 1946 in the Ear Lake area on the west side of the Coast Mountains south of Whitesail Lake. One of Cominco's 1945 prospecting crews had located mineralization in outcrops on the mountains around the lake, so the company wanted George and Rupert to prospect the area in more detail. Russ Baker flew in with food supplies a few times during the summer. George and Rupert found gold mineralization on the northwest side of Ear Lake. It was not of sufficient quantity for Cominco's operations, but it was large enough for George to stake a claim. When they returned home, George and Rupert brought with them logs for a new cabin with two rooms that Rupert constructed. George built a brick chimney for it. The cabin was rented to tourists and brought in some additional income. That summer, George and Else finally had their property officially surveyed, with the work done by J. A. Rutherford, a surveyor from Smithers.

In the fall, Rupert and his father went trapping, and they received just over $300 for the furs they harvested.

The family relationship changed again in 1947. Rupert obtained his first employment on his own, working on a federal government topographic mapping survey that was covering the area around the Coast Mountains near Tahtsa and Eutsuk Lake. There were three crews and they hired a few young local men who had outdoor skills and knew the geography of the area. For Rupert, this was the beginning of a career in surveying that lasted over forty years. Gloria finished grade 8 at Wistaria and wanted to continue her education. For grade 9, she attended school in Smithers because she was able to stay with a family that Else knew. For grades 10, 11 and 12, Gloria went to school in Burns Lake. With George and Rupert working, the family was able to pay for her boarding costs.

Else contributed to the family's income by writing some stories and doing translation work. As part of her involvement in the literary world, Else began a correspondence that year with the well-known and controversial American poet, Ezra Pound. Their exchange of letters lasted several years.

George wanted to explore the mineral potential around Ear Lake in more detail, so he applied to the BC government to upgrade the trail from Whitesail Lake into Ear Lake for more extensive prospecting. (A couple of Ootsa Lake residents had traplines around Ear Lake.) On July 15, 1947 the Minister of Mines reported to Cabinet that "he has authorized the expenditure of the following sum from the public moneys of the Province to facilitate the operation and development of the under-mentioned mining property, the said sum not to exceed fifty per centum of the cost of such work: Whitesail Lake–Ear Lake trail to Gamsby Group. Omineca Mining Division. $600." This was part of the government's "Grants in aid of mining roads and trails" program.

One of the major post-war changes in the economy of Wistaria and many other parts of the British Columbia interior was the development of the forestry industry. During the six years of war, many infrastructure projects had been postponed. The railroads had many ties that needed to be replaced. There was a housing boom in North America, and lumber was being shipped to Europe to help with rebuilding there. The rapid expansion of the forest industry in British Columbia was made possible by the establishment of portable sawmills that could be set up close to the timber. The development of chainsaws in the 1940s enabled timber to be cut much more quickly than by crosscut saw or axe. Logging provided income for several people at Wistaria as the trees on the forested land between Ootsa and François Lake were cut down.

George got a logging contract in the fall of 1947, and Rupert assisted him. Else wrote to Gloria on November 16: "Rupert got his power saw. They are just cutting up the big trees on the lake, it's wonderful! In 5 minutes the work of an hour with the cross cut saw. Daddy handles it too and smiles! They start logging tomorrow, both 500-600 dollars a month!" Rupert was one of the first people in the area to own a power saw. He also used it for cutting the family's firewood, which gave George more time to work on projects around the house.

The logging continued during the winter. In a letter to Gloria on February 15, 1948, Else wrote that George and Rupert would "come home for a week and will get a team of horses!! Heavy work horses! What do you say now? But then they do this work all alone." She noted that: "We got 10 rolls of barbed wire and fenced in more than 50 acres [20 hectares] where the horses can graze the whole summer and put in 10 acres [4 hectares] or more in oats for winter—when they will be in the lumber camps working. Hope this will end good and I have not to attend to them." Else commented that cars were becoming more common in the area and that "as soon as we have enough money Rupert will get one! [Rupert purchased his first car, a used one, in 1949.]" Gloria replied that "buying horses will certainly be an expense. However, it will be fine if we don't have to borrow horses all the time."

In another letter to Gloria ten days later, Else wrote in more detail about the purchase of the horses. George (along with Rupert) came home for a week and took "a team of horses from Bob Nelson, a big brown gelding, Alford breaks it in and his white mare from his team, about $250. He goes out in 2 days to Decker Lake to get heavy harness for them, another $100—you see how the money goes, but they need the horses and just leave them out if they do not use them. I refused to have anything to do with them, will not feed or water them! Can do it with the cows but not with such heavy horses." She also described the winter weather: "The last week before they came home I did not see one soul, the roads were drifted in, and the snow plow just came end of the week." She also wrote that Rupert cut "wood for Alford [Harrison] and Jimmy Nelson for 2 days. Everybody likes to have him with his engine [chainsaw]!"

The horses were used primarily for clearing the acreage that George leased from the government. The hay grown on this land was used to feed both the horses and cattle. The horses also ploughed the garden and were used occasionally in winter logging.

In her reply to Else, Gloria talked about the changes she had experienced during her time at school: "I have learned a lot in more than one way since I came to Smithers, both from a social and educational standpoint. And I have lost that shyness I used to have around people, and I am certainly glad for that."

On March 4, Else wrote that George and Rupert remained at home a second week, and "all the money has to go for the team and harness and shingle trees, logging chains etc, more than $400 and nothing left for us, even the grub bill we have to pay from the bank account. Hope you have enough money to come home [during Easter] or I have to send you some from my own account." While George and Rupert were back they made some repairs in the kitchen and during the second week Jim Nelson took Rupert "up in the sleigh for 3 days to cut all their wood [Jim Nelson lived on property on the benchland above Ootsa Lake]." A week later, Else wrote that "at last they got the 2 big horses, the harness and made a sleigh and went off galloping Tuesday to the wood camp. This time they should make good money as they get it all alone now and Bill H is not there."

After Easter, Else wrote to Gloria.

> Wed[nesday] Rupert and Papa stopped the logging and came out. They made about 60,000 ft [18,000 metres]. Thursday I went with Daddy at 8 o'clock sharp, our team galloping all the

> 10 miles [16 kilometres] to the camp. We loaded up everything and then I cooked coffee and the truck with a load of planks for the culvert arrived with Cliff, Billy and Nuckey [Else's nickname for Rupert] and we all had lunch together. Later we went to Jacob Lund's camp and took some more stuff and home again just around 4 o'clock. It was a nice outing, my first one and I hope not the last one!

At the end of the letter, she wrote: "We are getting 2 truckloads of lumber tomorrow and then 2 more! Big piles of lumber for us. Building horse barn at first, you will not see the old barn again. The best lumber will be for the new house." The first cabin for tourists had been a success, so they constructed a second one. In addition, some of George's family planned to come for a visit and they needed more accommodations for them.

In mid-April, Else wrote to Gloria, describing conditions around their place: "All this week they [George and Rupert] cut fence posts and brought in 2 loads every day! Over 400 posts and some rails. The roads are all mud, no traffic allowed, no cars either, just the mail truck and some jeeps! Tomorrow Rupert starts cutting our firewood and Daddy is hacking the old barn to pieces!" Later in the spring, they hired a man to clear an acre of land, and in

Rupert (right) and Major West (centre) on the federal government's topographic survey. University of Victoria Archives 4-6-51

mid-May Else wrote to Gloria that "Daddy was disking and burning all the brush piles; the land sure looks like a farm now." As part of the expansion of their farm, George applied for and received from the BC government a second lease of a parcel of land for hay and grazing purposes.

In June, Rupert returned to work on the government topographic survey for a second summer. He had a few offers of local work for the summer, but Else felt that he should have employment where he learned a skill.

George spent the summer prospecting, and wrote a report to the Department of Mines describing the work that he did at Ear Lake and in the surrounding area.

> **Prospecting Report of the summer 1948**
>
> I spent 2 months prospecting the Ear Lake–Kimsquit Territory. Prospected at Lindquist–Ear Lake Pass. Discovered one vein copper and iron, but assays only ran 8% in copper and no gold values.
>
> Then I went across Ear Lake making for granite contact on Catsquit Mountain. On the southwest end of Ear Lake where granite contact intrudes I found a sample which went gold, trace, silver nil.
>
> Crossed a mountain from Ear Lake over to Kimsquit Lake. Prospected north side of Kimsquit Lake when I found a quartz lead, one half mile and 6 feet in dimension. It contained mineralized termination, molybdenum, pyrite and copper. I had not much time to explore further as the weather turned very bad.
>
> Crossed at the foot of Kimsquit Lake and took several assays on the south side of the lake but they were of little importance. Mineralized quartz in evidence on Foresight Mountain.
>
> I spent 2 weeks in the Sibola Rand [Ranch] where I staked 4 claims...—It was recorded at Burns Lake on September 14th, 1948.

The two weeks that George spent staking claims in late summer was for the Lead Empire group. This was in the Sibola region on the north side of the Tahtsa River. The initial claims were staked in 1929 for Consolidated Mining by George's friend, Bill Sweeney, who had died. H. C. Hughes, who had been a mining engineer for Cominco at the nearby Emerald Glacier mine in 1929 and had visited the site, informed geologist William Patmore about the potential value of the claims. Cominco had allowed the claims to lapse, so the restaking was headed by William Patmore, with Fred Sanft as promoter. George was hired to help locate the original mining claim boundaries. Although he had not been involved in staking the initial claims, George knew the area well, and Bill had described where the claims were located.

In a letter on September 20 Sanft wrote:

> According to the information from Mr. Hughes, there is no doubt that the property you staked at Tahtsa is the real thing. Please send along the records at your earliest convenience.
>
> The assays on the Tahtsa are all good, from $75 to $100 per ton silver, lead & zinc. One of the veins ran $5 in gold, 104 oz [3 kilograms] silver, 8% lead. George, this confidential information for you. Use it to your advantage if you see fit.

In an article titled, "Lead Empire (Omineca) Group" that he wrote for the February 1949 edition of *Western Miner,* Patmore described the situation.

> During the summer of 1948, the writer was sent into the Tahtsa–Nanika Lake area, Omineca Mining Division, by G. F. Sanft, to locate a lead-silver-zinc deposit staked by the late Wm. Sweeney in 1929 and since forgotten. Original knowledge of the find was transmitted through the courtesy of Mr. H. C. Hughes, now engineer for the Government Mines Inspection branch, but formerly employed by the Consolidated Mining and Smelting Co. in that district.
>
> While searching for the old showings, it was the writer's pleasure to discover for his principal, Mr. Sanft, two promising separate deposits of similar minerals, adjacent to the initial ore zone and marginal to a hitherto unmapped stock of intrusive grandodiorite.

He wrote about the claims, their history, and their location.

> At present there are three groups of claims all owned by Mr. G. F. Sanft. The original group, "Tri Connell" mineral claims, was relocated as the "Lost" group by the writer's aide, Mr. George Seel, of Wistaria, B.C., who acted as agent for Sanft. The other two were staked by the writer as the "Fissure" and "Silver" Groups for Mr. Sanft. Each group contains four claims centered on the showings, and the adjacent ground for many miles in all directions is available for staking if desired...
>
> The three groups, now termed collectively the "Lead Empire," lie within one and a half miles [2.4 kilometres] of

> each other on the watershed of Tahtsa–Nanika and Kid Price Creek near Ootsa Lake in the Omineca Mining Division.

While George and Patmore were staking claims, Sanft remained at the Seel home. Else noted that "he even helped to bring in the hay when George had to leave in the middle of haying season. So the three of us amused ourselves. The promoter often took us for drives in his big, new car. We picnicked at different lakes, fished, and visited the Dutchman [Klaverwyden]."

Over the winter George and Rupert went logging again. On February 24, Else wrote to Gloria: "Daddy and Rupert home for 2 days and both had a terrible cold! The whole camp was sick with the flu and they could not work in the cold—we had again 40 below zero. They hardly made enough money to pay for their board! And they will not get paid before spring! By then it will all be spent, as there is nearly $200 to pay for the land. Rupert had engine repairs and shoes, pants, etc. 3 parcels—$50—So goes the money." In June, Gloria wrote to Else: "I saw all the logs that Rupert and Daddy helped cut this winter at Nadina, there. The entire bay was almost covered."

One of the cabins built for guests. Else Seel photograph. University of Victoria Archives 4-6-49

In the rejuvenated postwar economy of British Columbia, the provincial government resumed consideration of a large hydroelectric project along the Coast Mountains. From the surveys they had conducted during previous years, the provincial government believed that the most feasible project would be on the headwaters of the Nechako River. A dam would be constructed below the Great Circle of lakes of the upper Nechako in the vicinity of the Grand Canyon of the Nechako River. It would create a large reservoir of water. At the western end of the reservoir, along the western

The Seel house in the late 1940s, with Ootsa Lake in the background. Else Seel photograph. University of Victoria Archives 3-35-47

shore of Tahtsa Lake, a sixteen-kilometre tunnel would be constructed that would drop 800 metres to sea level at Kemano on Gardner Canal. Turbines would utilize the energy of this water to create electricity, and a power line would carry it to the town of Kitimat, a deep-sea port on the Pacific Ocean where the electricity could be used for an industrial project. E. T. Kenney, MLA for the Skeena district, and minister of Lands and Forests, was one of the key government members for this project.

At the end of 1947, Boss Johnson became premier of British Columbia, and the next year the provincial government approached Alcan Aluminum regarding the construction of an aluminum smelter at Kitimat. Alcan expressed interest in the project. In March 1949, the provincial government passed the Industrial Development Act, which enabled Alcan to gain control of the necessary land and water.

In spring 1949, Alcan began to investigate the feasibility of building a smelter at Kitimat. Many local people were hired, including George and Rupert. George received fifteen dollars a day to work on the Tahtsa River. Else wrote in a letter to Rupert on June 26 that "Daddy and George Young came down with the boat on Wednesday to get more caps for the blasting. But they had to stay 2 days here on account of the terrible wind. Just could not make it. So they went off Friday evening, still very windy. Saturday we had rain and hail and the wind had blown itself out." Rupert received twenty-five dollars a day for freighting with his own boat and engine.

In the summer he worked for BC International Engineering, the company surveying the potential dam site. He was involved both with the surveying and the transport of men and equipment. During the summer, as the people along Ootsa Lake saw the activity that was occurring, they started to realize the impact the Kemano project would have on their way of life, and its inevitability. In October, Alcan representatives came to Wistaria and met with residents to explain the project.

George spent part of the summer doing more work for Fred Sanft on the Lost Group. He wrote a letter to Fred on October 9 summarizing his activities:

> I finally got back from the "Lost Group." I had two weeks of fine weather while I was out, the rest just rain. It took a lot of time every morning packing and going up 1500 feet [457 metres] as there is no wood or shelter within 1 ½ miles [2.4 kilometres] of the claim and it takes 2 days to reach camp from Tahtsa Lake with a pack.
>
> I managed to get a cut in on the ore showing 15 feet high [4.57 metres] at the back. I did not get down to bedrock on account as it was caving in all the time, but plenty of ore is

Leaving for a prospecting trip to relocate the mining claims for the Lost Group. University of Victoria Archives 4-6-09

> coming out all the time, it is the same grade as the samples Patmore took. The vein seems to be six feet wide [2 metres] or more. I did not bring any samples out as you had not written about this before that you wanted some. I also noticed a lead at the bottom cutting in on the glacier which I think is the same one as it is in a straight line. No one has been in that vicinity this season outside myself and your other groups are safe in case you want them again sometime.

After completing the work for Sanft, George did some more work on the Tahtsa River. Then he went trapping for a short time. Ominously, he returned with shortness of breath and with the rheumatism in his wounded knee bothering him.

William Patmore sent Else this photograph of himself at Gibraltar Mine in the early 1970s. He received an undergraduate degree in geology at the University of British Columbia and a graduate degree at Princeton. Patmore's staking of the Lead Empire claims later led to a court case, and, although he was not convicted, he had to pay court costs. Patmore was a defendant in several other court cases related to mining ventures and was arrested once as a suspect in a bank robbery. Eventually he was expelled from the Association of Professional Engineers. Seel family collection

In Memoriam

The headwaters of the Nechako was the main source of water to be used for generating power for the Alcan project. But the British Columbia government also offered Alcan a small secondary source. About five kilometres northwest of Tahtsa Lake and across a range of mountains lay Nanika and Kidprice lakes. From the outlet of Kidprice Lake, the Nanika River flowed into Morice Lake, which is on the Skeena River drainage. Alcan received permission to construct a dam at the outlet of Kidprice Lake, creating a reservoir in the valley of the two lakes. A tunnel could be built from the upper end of Nanika Lake to Tahtsa Lake. Since Nanika Lake was higher in elevation, gravity would cause the water to flow into Tahtsa Lake.

To determine the feasibility of this option, Alcan needed to do studies of water flow in the Nanika–Kidprice drainage. BC International Engineering decided to begin this project in early 1950, during the winter, and they hired George as one of the members of a small crew. The men flew into Kidprice Lake where they found that the snow was deep and the temperature cold, making it hard to establish a comfortable camp. Alongside the Nanika River, the crew dug a well down to below the level of the river to monitor the river flow. After working for about a month, the men returned in late March.

When George returned, Else noticed that he had lost a considerable amount of weight and was tired. He tried to rest and regain his health, but on April 1, he died at home, probably of a heart attack. George was buried at the small cemetery at Wistaria.

Else wrote a poem about George with both German and English versions. The original poem, written in German, is more detailed. The English version was included in *British Columbia: A Centennial Anthology*, published in 1958.

In Memoriam

By the edge of the forest
you built our house of logs.
No road, no path to mark the way,
reached by a boat alone.
I sang my German songs
but only squirrels listened.

Always you went away.

Watching from the window
I saw your little craft
merge into the horizon.
Or in the long cold winter
I awaited your return.
Over the gray ice you trudged,
strapped to your back
the packboard laden with fur;
dark, lustrous mink and marten,
ermine, a silver fox,
lynx or beaver.

And so passed many years.

The struggle for
our daily bread was hard.
The land to till
and the first furrow,
the seed to sow
and harvesting the crop.
The children learned to help so early:
to feed the animals,
to carry wood and water,
to pick wild berries
and to catch the fish.

Always I waited for your return.

There was your motor-boat
upon the lake. Weary you came
back from the mountains.
And from the packboard
you produced rock samples.
Glitter shone in the stone;
copper, silver, gold.
And in the evenings you spun
your tales around the fire;
of danger and adventure,
of Indians, trappers,
hunting of caribou and grizzly bear.

The waves pounded at our door.
The stars and Northern Lights
crowned our heads.
The wild geese honking
the eternal season.

Then for the last time
you came back.
Time had not spent you
Or taken your strength.
Smiling you laid down to sleep.
I held you in my arms,
and suddenly I felt the death,
The ender of all things.

And I wished I could have
gone with you.

IN MEMORIAM

Du warst mein Mann.
Fuer zweiundzwanzig Jahre
Telle ich mein Leben
Im Norden Kanada's mit Dir.

Am Urwaldrande bautest Du
unser kleines Hausa us Staemmen.
Kein Weg, kein Steg,
Im Boot nur zu erreichen.
Eichhoernchen hoerten
meine deutschen Lieder.

Und immer warst Du fort.
Und immer sah ich ueberm See,
das kleine Boot zu spaehn,
oder im langen, kalten Winter
uebers Eis Dich kommen.

Und aus dem Packboard
breitest Du die Felle,
glaenzend und dunkel:
Mink, Marder, Hermelin,
ein Silberfuchs, ein Lynx,
Otter und Biber.

Zweimal bracht ich
ein Kind nach Haus
und legte es in Deine Arme.
Fremd schien es Dir,
Unglaeubig namst Du
diese kleine Hand
und zaehltest die fuenf Finger.

So vergingen viele Jahre,
Unmenschlich schien das Muehen
um ein Stueckchen Brot,
das Land zu roden
und die erste Furche ziehn,

die Saat zu saeen
und die Frucht zu ernten.

Die Kinder halfen schnell
das Noetige zu tun,
die Tiere futtern,
Holz und Wasser holen,
die wilden Beeren pfluecken
und die Fische fangen.
Alles auf unserem Tische
kam von unserer Arbeit,
unserer Hand.
Und immer lauschte ich.
Das Surren des Motors,
da hielt das kleine Boot
vom langen Trip.

Und aus dem Packboard
kamen Bergskristalle,
die Erze, blitzen im Gestein:
Kupfer, Silver, Gold.

Am Abend folgten die Geschichten
Vom Lagerfeuer, von wilden
Und verwegenen Gestalten,
Von Indianern, Jaegern,
Elch-un Baerenjagden.

Die Wellen schlagen schnell
bis vore die Tuere;
die Sterne und das Nordlicht
leuchten ueberm Haupt;
die wilden Gaense ziehn
und kuenden wiederum
der Jahreseiten ewgen Wechsel.

So famest Du zurueck
zu letztenmal.
Nichts hatte Zeit.
Dir fortgenommen,
nichts Dir von deiner Kraft geraubt.

Mit einem Laechein legtest
Du Dich wie zum Schlafen.
Ich hielt Dich noch im Arm,
da spuerte ich den Tod,
den Abschless aller Dinge,
und hatte das Verlangen itzugehn.
Wahrlich, es war genug getan.

The grave of George Seel in the Wistaria cemetery. Jay Sherwood photo

The End of Ootsa

In the spring of 1950, McElhanney Surveying, which received a contract to do much of the surveying for the Alcan project, asked Rupert to become an employee of their company. From 1950 to 1953, he worked on all aspects of the project, both on the Nechako watershed, and for the infrastructure being constructed along the Pacific coast.

Gloria graduated from Burns Lake Secondary School in June 1950. In the fall she went to Victoria, where she attended Normal School, training to be a teacher. Else decided to go with her.

The boats that Rupert built for the Alcan project. Else Seel photograph. University of Victoria Archives 9-8-63

On December 29, 1950 Alcan signed an agreement with the BC government. It granted the company a water licence for forty-nine years that included both the upper Nechako watershed and the Nanika–Kidprice drainage. [Alcan never used the Nanika–Kidprice portion of its water licence, and in 1987 gave it back to the government. Today the area is a BC provincial park.] Alcan agreed to build one aluminum smelter at Kitimat, with the opportunity to construct two additional ones in the future. The boundaries of Tweedsmuir Park were altered to accommodate the project. Land in the northern part was taken out, while additional land was added to the southern section, but the park became about a third smaller.

In 1951 construction began. This was the first large-scale hydroelectric project in central British Columbia, and it contained several components. The Kenney Dam, an earthen rock-filled dam 95 metres in height and 450 metres wide at the top, would be built across the Nechako River below the Great Circle of the upper Nechako. It would flood all of the lakes except Eutsuk and create the Nechako Reservoir with a surface area of 1200 square kilometres and a storage capacity of 7100 million cubic metres of water. A tunnel 16 kilometres long, 7.6 metres wide, and with an 800-metre fall, built at the western end of Tahtsa Lake, would divert the Nechako water to the Pacific Ocean. Using the force of the falling water, a powerhouse, built near the bottom of the tunnel would generate electricity. This electricity would be sent by a transmission line to Kitimat, 82 kilometres away. The project would create the community of Kitimat, at the head of Douglas Channel, where the smelter was to be built, and a small community at Kemano, on Gardner Canal, where the power would be generated.

Alcan also started the process of acquiring the land from people who lived along Ootsa Lake. The government had the power of expropriation, so the residents had to try to negotiate the best price that they could. Else sold the property in early 1951. She returned in the summer of 1951 and packed. Initially, she thought about staying at Wistaria. Part of the land leased for hay would not be affected by the flooding, so Rupert moved the tourist cabins there. However, Gloria remained in Victoria. Rupert was still at Ootsa, but would be moving to Vancouver, the head office for McElhanney, once the project was completed. By the end of the summer, Else decided to leave Wistaria and used the money she received for her property towards the purchase of a small home in Vancouver.

Residents along Ootsa Lake were not the only people to be displaced by the project. The dam had no provision for release of water. This was to be done through the Skins Spillway, which was constructed farther west along the reservoir that would be created by the dam. A channel was dug to Skins Lake, the headwaters of the Cheslatta drainage that ran through Cheslatta and Murray Lake, and entered the Nechako River downstream from the Grand Canyon. This would provide Alcan with an easy way to release excess water. However, it would require the relocation of the First Nations people who lived along this waterway. The Cheslatta Nation had three reserves along Cheslatta Lake. Water would not be released through the spillway until the reservoir was filled. In the meantime, the federal Department of Fisheries was concerned about a lack of water for salmon in the Nechako River. Alcan constructed a temporary dam at the outlet of Murray Lake to hold back some water that could be released into the Nechako during the summer months. This necessitated the removal of the Cheslatta people from the reserves where they lived. In April 1952, the Cheslatta were given just two weeks to leave, and they received minimal compensation for the loss of their homes, fields and trapline territories. The Department of Indian Affairs did almost nothing to protect the rights or promote the welfare of the Cheslatta people, who were moved to land farther north around Grassy Plains. (In 1993, the Cheslatta First Nation received additional compensation, and in 2012, Rio Tinto Alcan gave them 4,500 acres [1821 hectares] of land located in their traditional territory.)

Workers constructed a tunnel that diverted the Nechako River around the Kenney Dam site. In the spring of 1952, the construction of the dam began. Kenney Dam was completed by the fall; the diversionary tunnel was closed; and water started to back up behind the dam, creating the Nechako Reservoir.

Below the dam, the Nechako River began to recede, and water flow from the upper Nechako ceased until the reservoir was filled, over four years later. The Prince George *Citizen* published an article on October 9, 1952 mourning the loss of the river: "The mighty Nechako River officially died at twenty-seven minutes after ten o'clock yesterday morning. Shrouded with secrecy, a crew of workmen at the Kenney Dam sealed off the cavernous tunnel through which the river has been diverted during construction period. Officially, the Nechako River runs no more." The article described some of the effects that the lack of water would create.

In Vanderhoof, Norman Kerr, owner of the community's newspaper, and Rich Hobson, the famous author and cowboy, climbed down to the Nechako River downstream from the dam and watched it recede. Kerr wrote a passionate editorial, framed by a black border, that he published in the *Nechako Chronicle* on October 11, 1952.

OBITUARY

Passed away on October 8, 1952, at 10:27 am, the ageless and mighty Nechako River.

The passing, which brings great sorrow to residents of the Nechako Valley, was slow and agonizing to the tens of thousands of minnows, trout and the few salmon trapped in pools along the gravel banks as the waters slowly receded.

The incident may well mark the first time in history such a large and majestic river has been so suddenly and completely stilled at its source in the name of progress. The passing, due to the intervention of man, has destroyed forever a thing of beauty and divine creation...

Kerr then described the effects that the loss of the river would have on wildlife and the community.

Above the dam, the residents were gone, and any remaining buildings that would be affected by the reservoir had been burnt. The water level slowly and inexorably rose. Some people wrote articles or poems describing their feelings. Else wrote a poem about a farewell visit with a person who had been a friend and an important part of the community. (She wrote both an English and German version, which are slightly different from each other.)

The flooding of Ootsa, 1953. University of Victoria Archives 4-6-61

THE POSTMASTER
by Else Seel

The postmaster was the first to come.
He gave this place a name,
Looked in the seed catalogue
And found: Wistaria.

There followed two dozen families.
Men tilled the soil,
Women bore the children,
A log house for school
A log house for church
And a community hall.

The postmaster was the centre of things;
A tall and blond giant,
Good humored and stuttering,
Laughing heartily,
He swung his post marker
Like a hammer
On the outgoing mail.

He knew the children
And tossed the parcels
Into their outstretched hands.

Rain and shine,
Summer and winter,
Year in and year out
Came the mail to Wistaria.

We all met in the post office,
Said "Hello" and discussed the latest.
The postmaster was always there,
Laughing, stammering: "Just so, just so"

His hair became white,
His toothless mouth
Could no longer bite an apple,
But always friendly
He stamped the mail
And handed it to us.

The children grew up
And went away.
He stamped their letters.

We danced in the hall,
The whole night through,
The postmaster with us.

The old folks died
And we buried them.
The postmaster looked on.

A dam was built,
We had to leave our farms;
The postmaster too.

We went away,
The postmaster,
Leaning upon his cane
Said "Good bye" for the last time.

Der Postmeister
Else Seel

Der Postmeister kam zuerst.
Er gab unserm Ort den Namen,
sah in den Samenkatalog
und fand die blauweisse
Blutentraube: Wistaria.

Es folgten zwei Dutzend Familien.
Maenner rodeten Land,
Frauen gebaren die Kinder,
Ein Blockhaus fuer Schule,
ein Blockhaus fuer Kirche
und eine Community Halle.

Der Postmeister sah alles entstehn;
ein langer und blonder Riese,
gutmuetig stotternd,
laut lachend,
schwang er den Stempel
wie einen Hammer
auf die ein- und ausgehende Post.

Er kannte die Kinder
und reichte Pakete
in ihre ausgstreckten Haende.

In Regen und Sonne,
im Sommer und Winter,
jahraus und jahrein,
kam die Post nach Wistaria.

Wir trafen uns in dem Post-office
sagten "hallo" und erzaehlten das Neuste.
Immer sass der Postmeister dabei,
lachte und statterte: "Just so, just so."

Sein Haare wurden Weiss,
sein zahnloser Mund

konnte keine Aepfel mehr beissen;
doch unentwegt freundlich
stempelte er die Post
und reichte sie uns.

Die Kinder waren erwachsen
und gingen fort;
er stempelte ihre Briefe.

Wir tantzen in der Halle
die ganze Nacht.
Der Postmeister dabei.

Die Alten starben
und wir begruben sie.
Der Postmeister dabei.

Wir holten die letze Post,
wir sagten das letze "Hallo",
der Postmeister dabei.

Wir gingen fort.
Der Postmeister,
auf seinem Krueckstock gestuetzt,
winkte zum letzenmal

Now everything is under water, 1956. Our property—25 years of work gone! University of Victoria Archives 4-6-61

The Alcan project displaced about eighty households along Ootsa Lake. Residents who lived on the benchland above the lake received no compensation, and were left with much smaller communities that lacked many of the organizations that they used to have. About seventy five Cheslatta people were displaced, along with a few farmers who lived in the Cheslatta drainage. Else wrote a poem about the sense of loss that most of the people felt.

Many of the settlers displaced from Ootsa Lake settled in the region around them. This was partially because of their connection to the area, and partially because the compensation they received was only sufficient to afford property that was available in the region. Else was one of the few people who moved directly to a large urban centre like Vancouver. Having lived in Berlin for many years, she was familiar with life in a large city.

Gloria completed her Normal School program, but never became a teacher. She worked for about a year before marrying. A few years later, she and her husband moved to Great Britain, where they lived for the rest of their lives.

During the time that he surveyed on the Alcan project, Rupert met Winnie Apps, the last teacher for the school at Ootsa Lake. They married after a courtship of several years. Rupert worked for McElhanney Surveying for over forty years and lived in the Vancouver area. He was involved in many important projects in BC, along with the proposed hydroelectric development on the Mekong River in southeast Asia in the 1960s and a mapping project in Nigeria. Rupert retained his father's trapline for many years, and spent part of his vacation during the winter trapping. In retirement, Rupert took geology courses, spent time prospecting, and has formed his own mineral exploration company.

Else continued writing during her years in Vancouver and was actively involved in the German community. She also worked with Rodney Symington, from the University of Victoria, who helped get more of Else's writing published. Else died in 1974 and her writing is recognized for its contribution to German-Canadian literature. George has Seel Lake named for him, located in the area where he spent much of his time trapping and prospecting, and where he felt most comfortable in the world. The claims that he staked on nearby Swing Peak are still active today and are held by his grandson. The Seel homestead on Ootsa Lake has been submerged under the Nechako Reservoir, but Else's diaries, photographs, and other documents about her and George help recount the story of life among the lakes and mountains on the headwaters of the Nechako during the first half of the twentieth century.

The Buyer

This play is cruel,
It's cat and mouse:
The victim of the flood
And you the buyer.

Indeed you buy.
You buy my life,
The best and biggest part of it,
The happiness and love,
The children and the close-knit family,
The log house and the wilderness.
You buy—how much, how much?

You buy the sun and moon,
How much, how much?
The garden and the picket fence,
The iris, lilacs and the hops.
How much, how much?
You buy the changing season,
The wild goose cry,
The neighbors, friends,
The whole community.
How much, how much?

Nothing remains.
A lifetime's work,
The peace of mind,
The satisfaction—
All gone.
You bought it all.
A paltry sum inflated money
For all the treasures of the world.

My roots, my home are gone.
I am a wanderer again.

Appendix

Coroner's Inquiry for John William Grell

The initial document was from the Burns Lake detachment of the British Columbia Provincial Police on July 4, 1927.

> The following is a statement taken from Mr. John Henry Dawson of Topley B.C. in connection with the boat accident on the Tahtsa River on or about the 28th day of June 1927 in which he and William Grell were thrown into the river on account of the boat capsizing resulting in William Grell being drowned.
>
> My name is John Henry Dawson c/o W. H. North, Taylor's Mine, Topley, B.C. Occupation—Prospector.
>
> On or about the 28th day of June 1927 myself and William Grell left George Seel's upper camp coming to Blue Lake. Some 6 miles below said camp in very bad water we struck log jam about 1 mile below camp and capsized throwing both of us into the water. This was about 2 pm.
>
> I crawled out on to the log jam while Grell was carried away to the other side of the river and the last I saw of him was hanging on to the willows apparently safe. A moment afterwards I saw the body going end over end down the current. Two days afterwards I was taken off by George Seel. The next day we found that the boat was high and dry on an opposite jam. We looked over the log jam for Grell's body but could not find the body.
>
> The next morning Seel and I looked over three or four log jams below discovering his hat and provisions and other things we had in the boat on the same side that he was last seen.
>
> Several of the articles were picked up by myself and Geo. Seel. We arrived at Wistaria on the 1st day of July and endeavoured to report same but could not get in touch with the police on account of the phone system.

After Grell's body was found in the Tahtsa River, the information was reported to the BC Provincial Police in Burns Lake.

Report by G. A. Johnson, Constable in charge of Burns Lake detachment, British Columbia Provincial Police
September 27, 1928
Re: William Grell: Drowned Tahtsa River B.C.

On September 19, 1928 I was informed by telephone from Ootsa Lake that a party of Indians travelling up the Tahtsa River had located the body of a man floating in the water and fastened there by willow branches.

The body was thought to be that of William Grell who was drowned in the Tahtsa River in the latter part of June 1927.

I immediately got in touch with Coroner Hoskins at Smithers who instructed me to proceed to the Tahtsa River and if possible to bring the body down to Ootsa and if not to bury same.

I left Burns Lake on the morning of Sept. 20th 1928 and found the body and buried same on the 24th Sept 1928 and returned to Burns Lake Detachment on the 26th September, 1928.

I was accompanied on the patrol from Ootsa by Mr. Edward van Tine and received assistance from Mr. H. J. NcNeil of Burns Lake. When we located the body (Mr. Van Tine and myself) on the 24th September, 1928 it was about half a mile west of the Bolan [Bolom] cabin. The Tahtsa River forks here and we travelled up the right channel, the right channel splits and the body was found in a small channel on the left of the right channel. The body was partly covered with water and was held there by willow branches. The body was bare, with the exception of boots on the feet; the body was face down, head up stream and apparently had been caught in the willows by the deceased's braces, a part of which was found, together with the deceased's watch hanging to same—a Waltham. It was impossible to recognize the body, but Mr. Van Tine, who knew the deceased personally, stated the body was of the same height and build as William Grell and when the watch was found Mr. Van Tine recognized the watch as the one carried by the deceased.

The body was badly decomposed and when we started to pick it up fell to pieces. The body was in such a condition that it

> could not be brought into Ootsa Lake and a spot was picked out in a clump of spruce trees and the body was buried there—a cross marks the grave. The grave is up the right hand channel of Tahtsa River from Bolan's [Bolom's] cabin about half a mile up in a clump of spruce on the left hand side.
>
> Should the coroner not intend holding an inquiry and wish a statement from Mr. Edward Van Tine of Ootsa Lake, I will secure a statement from him as to the finding of the body and the identity of the watch.
>
> Might I suggest that a letter of thanks be sent to Mr. H. J. McNeil, Government Telegraph Agent, Burns Lake, for his assistance to the patrol. Mr. McNeil assisted with his engine across Ootsa Lake and would not accept any remuneration for his assistance.

Edward Van Tine wrote a statement for the British Columbia Provincial Police.

> My name is Edward Van Tine. I live at Ootsa Lake. I accompanied Constable Johnson on Tahtsa River patrol re John William Grell—deceased. On Monday, September 24th 1928 we found a body lying face down in the Tahtsa River at a point about 100 yards below big jam or half a mile above fork in main river or in the first left hand channel or the right hand channel above the fork at Bolan [Bolom] cabin.
>
> The body was badly decomposed but from the height, 5'4", the shape of the body and build I was sure beyond a doubt it was the body of William Grell. A Waltham was found which had a crossed-checked back attached to a piece of suspenders under the willows where Grell was lying. This watch I recognized as the one which Grell was carrying when he was drowned. The body was examined by Constable Johnson and myself, and no marks of violence was found. There is no doubt in my mind that Grell was drowned on the Tahtsa River.
>
> The body was badly decomposed and it was impossible to bring same out—in fact when the body was being moved same fell to pieces.
>
> The body was buried in the first clump of spruce in the right hand fork of the Tahtsa River above Bolan's [Bolom's] cabin on Monday, September 24, 1928, about 4 pm.

Grell's body was discovered by Chief Louie. He gave a statement taken by Constable Johnson on October 8.

> My name is Chief Louie. I am an Indian. I come from Cheslatta Lake. Tommy Jack and myself were going up Tahtsa River and was in right hand channel. Just below "hole-in-the-wall" we found white man face down in water, head up river. We put willow sticks over him so he not go away. We tell McGibbon to tell police. McGibbon he carry freight for mine.

Chief Louie's statement triggered a couple of letters from the coroner, Stephen Hoskins, to the province's Deputy Attorney-General. The first correspondence was on October 31.

> I have the honour to enclose statements taken touching the death and the finding of the body of the above named, who was accidentally drowned in the Tahtsa River in the month of June 1927.
>
> As the body was discovered by an Indian, I shall be pleased if you will inform me if I am authorised to pay to Chief Louie, the Indian who discovered the body, the customary sum of $5.00 for reporting his discovery. I feel it would be good policy to give the Indians a small reward for immediately reporting such discoveries as this.
>
> Will add, I find deceased came by his death on or about the 28th day of June, 1927, by accidental drowning. It did not appear to be necessary to hold a formal inquest in this case.

The second letter was on the last day of November.

> I am in receipt of a letter from the Indian Agent, Mr. R. H. Moore, of Vanderhoof, in which he states he understands there was a reward offered for the finding of Grell's body and reporting it.
>
> I have been unable to learn that any person locally offered any reward, and it is my opinion that the Government did not do so, but I believe there are precedents where the Government has made a donation of $5.00 to an Indian for reporting the finding of a dead body, and I believe it would be advisable to make an allowance to Chief Louie, the Indian of Cheslatta Lake, who reported the finding of Grell's body.
>
> I shall be pleased to learn your wishes in this matter.

Whether or not the Deputy Attorney-General heeded Hoskins' advice is unknown. It's apparent that a statement from George is missing from this inquiry. The day before Constable Johnson left Burns Lake, Seel had departed his home with a group of men to work on the Swing Peak mine. When travelling up the Tahtsa River they must have followed a channel that did not take them by Grell's body.

Sources Consulted

Archives

University of Victoria Archives

Else Lübcke Seel fonds SC111.

BC Archives

British Columbia Department of Lands and Forests, Lands Service
GR-0385.

Bureau of Mines photograph albums
198604-010, Volumes 27, 29, 30.

Grell, John William
GR-1321—Coroner's Inquiry, 1928.

Interviews
Cliff Harrison interview, AAAB1145.
Cyril Shelford interview, AAAB4078.
Living Memory: Homesteading at Ootsa Lake, AAAB3580.
People in Landscape: Journey to Ootsa, AAAB2671.

Northern British Columbia Fish and Wildlife Records
GR 1085—Trapline correspondence.

Parsons, T. W. S.
Diaries—MS1134; Photographs—198006-028.

Swannell, Frank
Diaries—MS392; Photographs—198002-017.

Water Rights Branch
GR-1024—Correspondence.

Cheslatta Archives

Government documents

BC Government. Order-in-Council #1415, 18th July 1946.

British Columbia Minister of Mines Annual Reports, 1926–1929, 1945.

"Certificates of Incorporation." British Columbia Gazette, November 10, 1927, 3599.

"Tweedsmuir Park, British Columbia, Canada." British Columbia Department of Lands. Victoria: King's Printer, 1938.

NEWSPAPER ARTICLES

Bella Coola

"The Stampede to Tahtsa River." *Bella Coola Courier*, September 27, 1913, 1.

Burns Lake

"Wm. Grell Loses Life in Rapids of Tahtsa River." *Burns Lake Observer*, July 7, 1927, 1.

"Capt. Irving Says Steamboats Feasible from Whitesail to Ootsa Lake Landing." *Burns Lake Observer*, July 28, 1927, 1.

"Quarter Million Dollars for Tahtsa Development Work." *Burns Lake Observer*, May 10, 1928, 1.

"Big Development Next Year on Seel Property at Tahtsa." *Burns Lake Observer*, November 1, 1928, 1.

"New Planes for B.C." *Burns Lake Observer*, February 7, 1929, 3.

"Big Staking Boom Hits District." *Burns Lake Observer*, August 15, 1929, 1.

"Grizzly Bear Attacks Mining Engineer on Sibola Mountain." *Burns Lake Observer*, September 12, 1929, 1.

"Wistaria Prospector Hurled Twenty Feet in Explosion." *Burns Lake Observer*, September 25, 1930, 1.

"George Seel Settled Here in 1914." *Burns Lake Review*, April 13, 1950, 1.

New Hazelton

"One Drowned, One Saved." *Omineca Herald*, New Hazelton, July 15, 1927, 1.

Prince George

"Wonderful Hunting in Ootsa Lake Country." *Prince George Citizen*, May 7, 1920, 7.

"High Grade Ore from the Seel Property Will Come Out by Plane" *Prince George Citizen*, September 12, 1929, 6.

"Upper Nechako drains as diversion tunnel sealed." *Prince George Citizen*, October 9, 1952, 1.

Winnipeg

"Notable Water Power Sites Found in BC: Engineers Foresee Possible 1,200,000 Horse-Power in Coast District." *Winnipeg Tribune*, July 29, 1930, 16.

BOOKS

Barr, David. *One Lucky Canuck*. Victoria: Trafford Publishing, 2004.

Blackwell, Alan. *70 Years Next to Paradise*. Self-published, 1998.

Calonego, Bernadette. *Under Dark Waters*, trans. Gerald Chapple. Seattle: Amazon Crossing, 2015.

De Zepetnek, Steven. *Comparative Literature: Theory, Method, Application*. Atlanta: Ropodi, 1998.

Giesbrecht, Jean Clark. *Heritage Lost: A People's History of the Ootsa Lake Region 1905–1955*. Likely, BC: Quesnel Lake Publishing, 1994.

Harrison, Alf. *A Glimpse of the Past*. Self-published, 2000.

Neering, Rosemary. *Wild West Women: Travellers, Adventurers and Rebels*. North Vancouver: Whitecap Books, 2000.

Seel, Else. *Canadian Diary: a Novel*, trans. Gloria Regina Reed. Seel family collection.

Seel, Else *Kanadische Tagebuch*. Erdmann, 1964.

Seel, Else. *Haus im Urwald*. Regina: Western Printers, 1956.

Shelford, Arthur and Cyril Shelford. *We Pioneered*. Victoria: Orca Book Publishers, 1988.

Shelford, Cyril. *From Snowshoes to Politics*. Victoria: Orca Book Publishers, 1987.

_____. *From War to Wilderness*. Victoria: Shelford Publishing, 1997.

Turkki, Pat. *Burns Lake & District: A History Formal and Informal*. Burns Lake: Burns Lake Historical Society, 1973.

Watters, Reginal Eyre, ed. *British Columbia: A Centennial Anthology*. Vancouver: McClelland and Stewart, 1958.

Wood, June. *Home to the Nechako: The River and the Land*. Victoria: Heritage House Publishing, 2013.

DISSERTATIONS

Beach, Christopher. "Beneath the Waters: A Microhistory of Ootsa Lake, a Northern Eurocanadian Community." M.A. thesis, University of Northern British Columbia, 1998.

ARTICLES

Bonnycastle, R. H. G. "Lord Tweedsmuir as a Mountaineer." *Canadian Alpine Journal* 28, No. 2 (1943): 53–60.

De Zepetnek, Steven. "The Life Writing of the German-Canadian Pioneer Else Seel (1894–1974)." *Melus* (Autumn 1996): 25–34.

Larsen, Soren. "Collaboration Geographies: Native-White Partnerships During the Resettlement of Ootsa Lake, British Columbia, 1900–52." *BC Studies* (Summer/ Autumn 2003): 87–114.

Patmore, W. H. "Lead Empire (Omineca) Group." *Northern Miner* (February 1949): 39–43.

Riedel, Walter E. "German Writing." *Canadian Encyclopedia*.

Symington, Rodney. "Else Seel: Survival Assimilation and Alienation." In *The Old World and the New: Literary Perspectives of German-speaking Canadians*, ed. Walter Riedel. Toronto: University of Toronto Press, 1984.

Tweedsmuir, Lady. "Tweedsmuir Park: a Canadian Pilgrimage." *National Geographic* (April 1938): 451–476.

Index

E

F

G

H